Coming to Peace:
Resolving Conflict Within
Ourselves and With Others

ALSO BY ISA GUCCIARDI, PH.D.

Return to the Great Mother (book)
(Isa Gucciardi, Ph.D., Sacred Stream)

The Four Immeasurables: Meditations on Equanimity, Loving-Kindness, Compassion and Joy (recording)
(Isa Gucciardi, Ph.D., Red Cow Records)

Sacred Drums for the Shamanic Journey (recording)
(Isa Gucciardi, Ph.D., and Laura Chandler, Red Cow Records)

Coming to Peace:
Resolving Conflict Within Ourselves and With Others

Isa Gucciardi, Ph.D.

with Laura Chandler

Foreword by Thupten Jinpa, Ph.D.

Sacred Stream Publishing

San Francisco

Sacred Stream

Sacred Stream, San Francisco, 94127
(415) 333-1434 | info@sacredstream.org | sacredstream.org

Printed in the United States of America

10 9 8 7 6 5 4 3 2 1

Ordering Information:
Special discounts are available on quantity purchases by corporations,
associations, and others. For details, contact the publisher.

Cover Design: Catherine Marick
Interior Design: Cody Humston, Simone Kershner
Cover Image: © Deborah Hall
Editors: Laura Chandler, Melanie Robins

ISBN-13: 978-0692705490
ISBN-10: 069270549X

Library of Congress Control Number: 2017932330

This book is dedicated to the Earth and all her beings.

CONTENTS

FOREWORD

It's such a joy and honor to have the opportunity to write these few words in the form of a foreword to this vitally important book by Isa Gucciardi, a dear friend whose work I have admired for a long time. Isa is best known for her innovation of the powerful technique of Depth Hypnosis, which integrates insights from Buddhist and contemporary psychologies with Native American Shamanic practices. Isa shares with the general reader for the first time, in this book, the insights she has gained through decades of experience with her clients, so that many others may be able to apply these insights in their day-to-day life. Drawing on powerfully moving stories of her clients, Isa shows how, if we choose, each of us can learn to live our life with courage, acceptance, and joy, instead of fear, anxiety, and self-doubt. She calls this "taking radical self-responsibility" for our wellbeing and the wellbeing of others. A central teaching in this book relates how to engage constructively with our suffering.

The reality of suffering and how should we deal with it have been, of course, important existential questions for us humans throughout the ages. The Buddha, for example, framed our entire spiritual quest in terms of the Four Noble Truths. Using medical analogy, the Buddha spoke of how *suffering* (ailment) exists, how suffering comes from its *origin* (conditions that cause sickness), how there can be a *cessation* of suffering (illness-free state), and, finally, how there is the *path* (the medicine) that brings about such true freedom. And a crucial part of that path, the Buddha revealed, has to do with gaining insight into how our own thoughts, emotions, and habitual tendencies often create the conditions for our own suffering. In broad terms, I would summarize the essence of this insight in the following way:

- It's through our perceptions—of ourselves, of others, and the world we live in—as well as the attitudes and values we bring into our engagement, that each of us literally creates the world we individually experience.
- Our perceptions shape our emotions, which, in turn, motivate our behavior towards ourselves, towards others, and the world around us.
- As sentient creatures, we instinctively shun pain; yet suffering is a defining character of our sentient nature. However, it's often our own resistance to suffering—through denial and suppression—that makes things worse and leads to further suffering.
- So a true path to freedom includes understanding our own mind based on genuine self-knowledge, as well as the ability to relate to our suffering with acceptance, without resistance and negative judgment. In brief, our happiness does not lie in avoiding pain and sorrow, but, rather, making peace with them and living our full human potential despite our suffering.

What is remarkable about Isa's book *Coming to Peace* is that it demonstrates powerfully how to apply these ancient universal insights to our very contemporary life. In everyday idiom and sharing transformative experiences of her clients, the author brings to life, in a powerful way, what it means to truly let go, develop genuine self-acceptance, and tap into the creative energy of suffering. The book shows us how, instead of being overwhelmed, we can allow our experience of suffering to enrich and empower us—to make us feel more connected with ourselves and others, to find meaning and purpose, and to teach us how to live fully with courage and joy. What Isa teaches in her remarkable book is a journey of mindfulness and self-acceptance—in short, true self-discovery through the path of compassion. This is a genuine offering to the world and I thank my friend for writing this important book.

May this book be a source of inspiration, courage, and healing to many who seek the path of compassion and peace through self-knowledge!

Thupten Jinpa, Ph.D.
Principal Translator to H.H. the Dalai Lama
Author of *A Fearless Heart: How the Courage to be Compassionate Can Transform Our Lives*

INTRODUCTION

It was one of those stereotypically foggy mornings in San Francisco when I sat for what felt like an eternity in the listless waiting room of my doctor's office. As the blue fluorescent lights buzzed overhead, I worked hard to calm my growing frustration. When the doctor finally entered the exam room two hours after my scheduled appointment time and said, as he had many times before, "Thanks for being so patient," I responded in bare honesty: "I may be a patient, but I am not sure I am patient."

Unfazed, the doctor quickly moved on, business as usual, and told me that I had an incurable autoimmune disease. Apparently my body was at war with itself. As I asked him about the medication I just learned I would have to take for the rest of my life, he stopped me mid-sentence and said, "You know, a lot of people who have this condition have experienced a major loss. Have you?"

It was the mid-nineties, and I was running a translation company at the height of the dot-com boom in downtown San Francisco, raising two small children, and running a complex household. I felt happy and fulfilled by my life. However, because I was dedicated to being there for my children when they got home from school, I did wind up working what amounted to two 40-hour workweeks: one in the daytime and one at night. I hadn't recognized the high levels of stress that trying to keep so many balls in the air had caused. But it was this pressure that had brought on my health problems.

The doctor's question continued to haunt me, so I set out on a quest to find out what it was that I had lost. As part of the process, I tried to figure out how I had not recognized this stress and the effects it had on me; I largely experienced my life as happy and fulfilling. This led me to notice a bigger pattern within me related to the dynamics of stress, which pointed to my childhood and the many conflicts I experienced growing up.

I knew that whatever was causing me to be sick lay somewhere beyond the borders of my conscious mind. To answer the question, *What had I lost?*, I turned to hypnotherapy. What I learned was that I had actually lost parts of my memory, and, therefore, parts of myself, in trying to endure what I came to understand as an unusually conflict-laden childhood. My parents and my older brother were almost constantly fighting with one another, and I generally tried to avoid all of them as much as possible.

Even though my experience with family members was primarily one of conflict, I felt fortunate to be living in Hawaii at the time, surrounded by the natural beauty of the land. Being outside and alone in such a paradise was, for me, like being in the presence of God. The sea, the wind, and the flowers were my constant companions. I spent hours in their company and the company of the many birds and crabs that inhabited the half-moon-shaped beach where I went to find peace, the place where the force of the waves would break against the rocks and spread out calmly over lava and sand.

Being with the spirits of nature, I could rest within myself. It was a puzzle to me why the order and peace I felt in nature was not something I had ever experienced with humans. I couldn't understand why no one else seemed to be tuning into the coherence and support of the natural world. I remember wondering what it was that kept my family members from sitting with the hibiscus and the ginger, as I often did, to feel whole and at peace.

When I entered kindergarten, I saw my classmates also struggling to relate to each other in a peaceful way. There was a lot of racial conflict among my multiracial peers. I was the only kid in the class not born on the island and I experienced a particular kind of prejudice from my classmates, but it wasn't just aimed at me. There was a great deal of conflict between all the children for one reason or another. Again, I could not understand why there was such disharmony when all around us the world of nature was largely at peace.

It was at that time that I started to wonder if there was any place on earth where the people were as peaceful as nature. I received the answer I'd been searching for when my family moved to Mexico and I was left in the care of a group of Huichol Indians. I discovered that the Huichols were more in synch with the rhythms of nature, which seemed to make them more tolerant and easier to be around. The ranch hands were patient as they taught me to ride horses, and the women cooking over open fires in the kitchen laughed warmly as they showed me how to mill corn. Frankly, it was disorienting to finally feel at home with people in the same way I did in nature.

Those experiences with the Huichol Indians fueled my resolve to find a way to bring the order and integration I felt with them and while in nature to others who might be feeling disconnected. I loved learning, and constantly read books about other cultures and traditions in an effort to discover more about people, like the Huichols, who kept their culture in tune with the earth, and the effect this harmony seemed to have on their way of being in the world.

When I was a young teen my family moved again, this time to Saudi Arabia, where the language and culture were completely foreign to me. I studied the nuances of the culture, learning as much as possible from my experiences. The big realization I came to by being exposed to the strictness of the Saudi culture is that all rules and laws are, fundamentally, arbitrary.

I specifically remember one afternoon, trying to navigate my way through the dizzying stench of blood hanging in the 110-degree heat after the weekly executions. My mind was full of questions as I tried to make sense of the brutality around me: *Why did so many people have to lose their hands for taking such small things? As far as I knew, this was not happening anywhere else; so why should it happen here? What was driving my family members to harm one another without a second thought? Why did my Hawaiian classmates, most of whom were from mixed bloodlines themselves, take such pleasure in excluding someone for looking different? And how had all of my differences not seemed to register with the Huichol Indians? What was it about them and the close contact they kept with the plants and animals that allowed them to maintain such harmony among themselves and with outsiders?*

These were the questions that drove me as I began my formal studies in the university setting and beyond. I studied linguistics and anthropology to try to find the culture that reflected the order of nature most perfectly. But I couldn't find one that fit the bill and was still extant, so I began studying comparative religion, trying to find the spiritual tradition that reflected the deep coherence I had always experienced in the heart of nature. This led me to study with indigenous artists and healers and to begin my formal study of Buddhism, first with Zen teachers and later Tibetan Buddhist teachers. I also studied transpersonal psychology to find a form of clinical practice that could bring the coherence of nature into the modern human experience.

My formal education spanned many years, and I spent much of that time working as a language translator, eventually running my own translation company. Life was also handing me lessons as I married and entered motherhood. Due to my experiences in childhood, I was determined to raise my children in a completely different way than I had been raised; I worked very hard to offer them the love and care they needed. Evidently, I had spread myself a bit too thin, which is how I ended up in the doctor's office that fateful day. As I set out on my healing quest, I continued to work and be a mother. My children were always central to my life, and I was determined to heal myself so that I could continue caring for them to the best of my ability.

As I worked to understand what it was I had lost due to the conflicts of my early life, I stumbled upon some deep insights about the way in which the experiences of my past were affecting the present. As I resolved the conflict between the parts of myself that were forgotten and the parts of myself that wanted to forget, I found my way out of my autoimmune disorder and was able to get off the medication once needed to manage it. And while I loved language and offering it as a bridge to others, I realized that I wanted to redouble my efforts to answer the question that had always presented itself to me: *How can we bring the harmony of nature into the conflicts of humans?* I sold my interest in the translation company and went back to school so that I could eventually begin a counseling practice.

My work in transpersonal psychology led me back to hypnotherapy, where I had started on my personal healing journey. Hypnotherapy interested me because of its effectiveness at helping people move beyond the conscious mind, where so many of us get stuck in our thinking. The subtler realms of consciousness are what held my attention because it is in these realms where deep change can occur. However, I found that the traditional hypnotherapeutic techniques used to help people address addictions, phobias, eating disorders, and other troubling issues, while helpful, were limiting. It wasn't until I combined the knowledge gained from my years of study and self-exploration into a therapeutic model called Depth Hypnosis, that I was able to help people make meaningful changes in their lives.

Depth Hypnosis is designed to help people transform deeply held patterns that contribute to a host of issues. It works with a person's presenting symptoms, whether they occur physically, mentally, emotionally, or spiritually, and sees those symptoms as a vehicle for self-exploration and understanding. By working with the body and mind in a holistic way and by working with altered states of consciousness in creative ways, people are able to access parts of themselves that are not usually available to them.

Depth Hypnosis arose in the clinical environment in response to the suffering of others. The insight behind its methodology emerged organically as I continued to reach beyond what I knew in order to help my clients. By the end of my first year in practice, I had so many people on my waiting list that I knew I could never see them all. I realized I had to teach others how to do what I was doing in order to meet the demand. This meant I had to actually articulate and define this process. I began teaching, and formed the Foundation of the Sacred Stream, a school for consciousness studies in Berkeley, California, in 2002. Through my work at the Sacred Stream and in one-on-one Depth Hypnosis sessions with clients, I have had the privilege of working with many inspiring people, and they are the reason I've written this book.

Coming to Peace is the conflict resolution model born out of my Depth Hypnosis counseling practice and the years of academic studies and personal healing work that I have just shared with you. With this book, I've attempted to walk you through the Coming to Peace process so that you can see how it's used to resolve conflict in groups (families, couples, etc.) and within individuals. You'll not only learn about the rich traditions that infuse this process and how it supports us in our busy, modern-day lives, but you will also see the process come to life through case examples.

It was because of my own journey across the effects of conflict into a more peaceful existence that I knew I wanted to help others do the same. The processes of Coming to Peace are at once esoteric and practical. It takes a bit of patience to understand them, but the potential rewards are far-reaching. With these techniques, I have travelled a long way into healing. My hope is that this book will interest others in doing the same and, in some small way, contribute to a more peaceful world.

Using This Book

Whether you are a spiritual seeker on a personal path or a mental health professional, *Coming to Peace* can help you better understand the ways in which conflict exposes the areas where we've become disconnected from others and ourselves. It also gives us a pathway out of the inner and outer turmoil that can cause us to become locked in joyless situations.

In Part I, you will learn about the roots of Coming to Peace in various wisdom traditions, the important role conflict plays on our journey toward wholeness, and how the process looks and functions. Parts II and III will help bring to life the process of Coming to Peace as practiced in Depth Hypnosis, using case studies and transcripts. Finally, Parts IV and V demonstrate how to put these practices into action.

Even if you never step foot in the office of a Depth Hypnosis Practitioner, the practices for cultivating peace and harmony described in this section will give you tools and encouragement for transforming your daily life into one that is increasingly more positive and enjoyable.

Disclaimer

Coming to Peace is not a guide to becoming a Depth Hypnosis Practitioner or mediator. While the practices are highly effective in helping people deal with personal difficulties and the methodologies quite straightforward, Depth Hypnosis is not a healing modality to be taken lightly. It is quite powerful and should only be used by someone who has undergone the appropriate professional training. Attempting to use Depth Hypnosis as it is explained in *Coming to Peace*, without proper training, is done so at one's own legal risk and at the risk of the wellbeing of one's clients.

If you are interested in learning more about Depth Hypnosis and training in the processes of Coming to Peace, please visit sacredstream.org or depthhypnosis.org.

A note about client stories and transcripts: In my attempt to illustrate in a vivid way just how the processes of Coming to Peace work, I have used amalgamations of client sessions throughout the book composed of personal stories and conversations. I have changed names, scenarios, and dialogues, combining different experiences to illustrate the process accurately while protecting client confidentiality. Any resemblance to actual persons, living or dead, or actual events or conversations is purely coincidental.

Lastly, on a style note, throughout the book "they" is used as a singular pronoun because it is gender neutral.

SECTION I

THE NATURE OF PEACE

CHAPTER 1: THE ROOTS OF COMING TO PEACE

"There can never be peace between nations until there is first known that true peace which is within the souls of men."

- Black Elk

We are all connected, through the air we breathe, the land we walk on, and the beauty of the earth that supports each one of us from the moment we are born until the moment we die. We are not separate from the earth, and we are not separate from each other. When we forget that, at our core, we all have the same primary yearning to be happy and live peacefully,[1] conflict arises. When we forget that others share this yearning, we move further away from our essential nature and become out of balance with everything around us, including those we love.

The resolution process of Coming to Peace is unique because it offers ways of mediating external conflicts with others, as well as methods for recognizing and addressing the places where we may be out of balance within ourselves. It is rooted in the wish for happiness that we all share, and holds the understanding that with conflict comes the lessons we need to learn. It does this by empowering us to tell the truth of our experience of conflict in a setting that is informed by the spirit and wisdom of thousands of years of experience. With the help of a specially trained practitioner, the process helps heal the hidden hurts that, unbeknownst to us, affect how we are in the world, those places where we have become severed from our connection to others and ourselves, and offers us a method for working through conflict with others in a way that is beneficial to all.

Many of us do not even recognize our connection to all living things and how fundamental it is to our happiness. It's hardly a surprise that we've forgotten this link when we consider the culture of war we live in, which has created so much devastation for so long. There are wars that pit nation-states against one another, wars that pit religions against one another, wars that pit genders against each other, the hidden wars we wage within ourselves, and the war against the earth caused by those seeking to profit from it. This last war is so remarkably damaging it's being called "the sixth extinction."[2] We can no longer deny the effects our disconnection from the earth, each other, and ourselves has on the world around us. Yet in the midst of all this conflict that degrades and splinters us, there is hope. We can find our way back to peace.

Coming to Peace is born out of my decades-long study of Buddhism and core mediation practices from a variety of earth-based wisdom traditions, as well as my counseling practice and life experience. In the early nineteen-nineties, I developed a counseling model called Depth Hypnosis[3] from which Coming to Peace evolved. Over the past twenty years, I have seen Coming to Peace help resolve conflict in families, business relationships, and even internalized conflict within individuals. I have witnessed the unique gifts Coming to Peace has brought to clients stuck in the pit of internal and external conflict. I have seen how the essence of resolution lies in the recognition of the deep and unbroken connectedness we share as human beings. Again and again, I have seen the processes of Coming to Peace meet those in conflict and provide them a path to reconciliation and wholeness.

To better understand how Coming to Peace works and how it's able to effect such profound healing, we must first look at its roots in some of the world's most ancient wisdom traditions. Buddhism, which emerged in the fifth century B.C.E. as the result of a young Indian prince's investigation into the nature of reality, informs the Coming to Peace process on a number of levels. While it is a religion with spiritual teachings, it is highly scientific and philosophical in nature, and no theological belief is required for someone to benefit from its methods for living a happier and more peaceful life. In fact, contemplative practices such as meditation and mindfulness, which are staples of Buddhism, already permeate our society. Stand in line at the grocery store and you'll likely see a magazine cover touting the many benefits of these ancient practices.

In recent decades, scientists have taken a great interest in and have begun studying the efficacy of meditation and compassion practices for outcomes such as stress reduction and an improved sense of wellbeing. In 2007, Buddhist scholar Thupten Jinpa, Ph.D., and neurosurgeon Jim Doty developed the Center for Compassion and Altruism Research and Education at Stanford University. CCARE provides an ongoing forum for scientists, psychologists, and other interested professionals to study the effects of altruistic behavior. According to Thupten Jinpa, CCARE has "helped place the study of compassion squarely within established science."[4]

Major corporations have also begun investing in programs that adapt mindfulness and other such practices, in an effort to increase productivity in the workplace. A notable example of this is at Google, one of the largest and most influential tech companies in the world. Chade-Meng Tan, a former engineer at Google, introduced a mindfulness-based emotional intelligence curriculum for the organization's employees called "Search Inside Yourself"—he later wrote a book about it by the same title. This program has had an immensely positive effect on the culture and work environment at Google, including greater creativity, productivity, and overall job satisfaction.[5]

These are just some examples of the ways that Buddhism is subtly influencing contemporary society in a positive way. As Jinpa suggests in his book, *A Fearless Heart: How the Courage to be Compassionate Can Transform Our Lives*, "If traditional Buddhist compassion practices touch us in fundamental ways that help nurture and develop our better self, clearly these traditional techniques can be translated into forms that we can all understand, no matter our race, religion, and culture. In other words, the deepest and best truths are universal."[6]

One of the most fundamental and pragmatic teachings to emerge out of Buddhist thought, and one that largely informs Coming to Peace, is The Four Noble Truths. These principles directly address the sources of conflict and hardship that we experience as human beings. They offer us an interesting way to look at life and how we experience it. For instance, these principles are based on the understanding that we all experience pain and hardship in our lives, which in most Buddhist translations is referred to as "suffering." If you've ever burned your hand on a hot stove or fallen in love with someone who didn't return your feelings, then you know what it means to suffer. But according to The Four Noble Truths, there is a way for us to navigate and even emerge out of our suffering, rather than be ruled by it. The first step in the liberation process is to understand the causes of suffering, which include aversion, attachment, and misunderstanding.[7]

Simply put, whatever we do not want is aversion. Whatever we want too much is attachment. And whatever we do not understand is misunderstanding or ignorance. All of these cause us to suffer. For example, if we are afraid to lose a friendship, and we clutch onto it despite having outgrown it, and the friendship ends, we suffer. Or, if we desperately want a new job and convince ourselves that it's the only job that will make us happy, and then we don't get it, we suffer. In fact, we suffer from not knowing that the time and energy we invest struggling with these strong attachments and aversions are causing us to suffer more than if we simply accepted the reality of the situation.

In this way, the Buddhist concept of suffering is a helpful framework for understanding our motivations in life and for initiating change. I have noticed over the years, with clients, students, and in my own life, how conflict can arise from the things we cling to, try to avoid, or misunderstand. In essence, all conflict is caused by this kind of suffering; and the Coming to Peace process wades into the dark places where we are choosing to engage in activities that create suffering for ourselves and others and helps us find a way out.

Coming to Peace also draws upon the equality and peace-generating practices of "earth-based wisdom traditions." These are the spiritual and educational systems practiced by peoples of the world who are now most

commonly referred to as "indigenous cultures." For thousands of
years, these practitioners have been nurturing relationships with nature,
guiding its power and wisdom to effect change in people's lives. The oldest
shamanic culture on record is that of the Australian aborigines, which dates
back over 150,000 years.[8]

Despite the losses these cultures have suffered through centuries of
colonialism, expansionism, and the usurpation of sacred lands, their
traditions continue to endure. In more recent times, there has been a
burgeoning interest in the practices of indigenous cultures, giving us the
opportunity to follow the traces of these traditions and learn what they
might offer us today.

Many indigenous cultures have spiritual belief systems and practices that
support conflict resolution among their members in a way that fosters
equality, and understands that, as humans, we all share common and similar
hopes, needs, and goals. As such, these traditions encourage and nurture
each person's ability to connect with this truth of common purpose when
they find themselves in conflict.

In Africa, *ubuntu* is a term used to describe the shared purpose, common
goals, and equality that comes from the Bantu language spoken throughout
many countries in Central, Southeast, and Southern Africa. It is a uniting
force among cultures in these areas and is recognized to have played an
important role in the restorative justice processes of the Truth and
Reconciliation Commission experienced in South Africa at the end of
Apartheid. In fact, the South African Constitutional Court stated that *ubuntu*
is "part of the deep cultural heritage of the majority of the population [and]
suffuses the whole constitutional order."[9]

In his article, "Race Apologies," University of Hawaii's Professor of Law
and Social Justice Eric Yamamoto further explains the relationship of
ubuntu to restorative justice practices:

> Restorative justice is reflective of the African notion of '*ubuntu*', or
> interconnectedness. *Ubuntu* is the idea that no one can be healthy
> when the community is sick. '*Ubuntu* says I am human only because
> you are human. If I undermine your humanity, I dehumanise

myself.' It characterizes justice as community restoration—the
rebuilding of the community to include those harmed or formerly
excluded.[10]

The same egalitarian approach to diplomacy and mediation practiced in
traditional African cultures was present in Native American
traditions, which was well documented by early European explorers and
ethnographers. The most consistent theme in their reports on the social
organization of the Native American tribes of eastern North America is one
of equality and freedom from social hierarchies. George Washington,
Benjamin Franklin, and other shapers of the United States were strongly
influenced by the governance espoused by the six tribal groups of the
Iroquois League.[11] In fact, in 1988, Congress passed Concurrent Resolution
331 recognizing the influence of the Iroquois League and other Indian
nations on the unification of the original Thirteen Colonies into one
republic, as well as the United States Constitution.[12]

In his book *Indian Givers: How Native Americans Transformed the World,* author
Jack Weatherford explains how during conflict resolution ceremonies the
Iroquois did not allow speakers to interrupt each other. And if someone
were to raise their voice, a period of silence would be prescribed.[13] Periods
of silence were also imposed after each speaker, in case they wanted to
refine or restate what they said. This was a radical change from diplomatic
circles of Parliament in England, during which everyone spoke at once and
attempted to out-shout each other when trying to come to
agreement. Europeans considered the Iroquois system of allowing each
member an equal voice revolutionary. According to Weatherford, the
overall intent of the Iroquois councils was to encourage unity at each step
through the informal discussion of an issue among equals.[14]

While members of the Iroquois League resolution circles were viewed as
equals, they did elect members to facilitate in the process. These leaders
were called "Pine Tree Chiefs"[15]—the Great White Pine, with its sheltering
branches is the symbol of peace and unity of the Iroquois League.[16] The
leaders not only helped those in conflict remain peaceful as they worked
through an issue, they also used ritual to support the members and the
process. For instance, in their "Edge of the Woods" ceremony, the Iroquois

would use a smoky fire to "clean off" or "clear" someone returning from an activity that caused them to act in a way that separated them from their essential nature. Such activities included war, hunting, and other things not peaceful in nature. As such, the Edge of the Woods ceremony was used before peace councils to prepare participants for the proceedings.[17] The use of a facilitator—and their supporting rituals—can be found in other indigenous traditions.

In Hawaii and other parts of the Pacific, in the resolution practice of ho'oponopono, a mediator called a *haku* was chosen to facilitate the process.[18] Meaning "to make good" or "to make right" in Hawaiian,[19] ho'oponopono is a healing process that addresses the underlying conflicts at the heart of social disease, political or religious conflict, and even physical disease in individuals.[20] Long ago, a *haku* was most often a *kahuna*, a spiritual leader and healer of the tribe. But today, a trusted elder from the group not involved in the conflict is more likely to serve as the facilitator.[21] To assist with ceremonies and other proceedings, *kahunas* would call upon helping spirits or totems.[22] And after clearing the ceremony space, they would say a prayer to ask for "guidance, strength, clarity, and healing."[23]

Historically, ho'oponopono was used to correct imbalances within family systems.[24] In her article, "To Set Right—Ho'oponopono: A Native Hawaiian Way of Peacemaking," Hawaiian and indigenous epistemology scholar and practitioner Manu Meyer explained ho'oponopono's main purpose: "Because each [family] member played an important role in the survival of the family, maintaining harmony was vital to keeping the family alive and well. Ho'oponopono was the means by which that harmony was maintained."[25]

In cases where a person was seeking help for physical illness, the *kahuna* would refrain from addressing the physical aspects of the illness until all aspects of the person's unseen experience were explored.[26] To facilitate this, the *kahuna* would call a meeting with the person's family and close community members. In this meeting, the *kahuna* would ask everyone if they were holding any grudges, fears, or judgments toward the person or if the person had any grudges, fears, or judgments that they were holding toward the community members.[27]

Every person affected by the conflict was given an opportunity to express their view without interruption in the resolution process of ho'oponopono, as crosstalk was not permitted.[28] Participants would go around the circle, peeling back the issue layer by layer.[29] If someone was disrespectful or became heated in any way, periods of silence called *ho'omalu* were prescribed for all parties—*ho'omalu* means "to bring under the care and protection of."[30] This period of silence gave participants time to reconnect with the spirit of truth and reflect on their experience before reengaging with the process.[31]

The essential elements of ho'oponopono, including prayer, discussion, confession, repentance, mutual restitution, and forgiveness, as well as self-scrutiny and discussion of individual conduct and group attitudes carried out in the spirit of *oia i'o*, or "the essence of truth,"[32] are as relevant today as they were in ancient Hawaii. Despite having gone underground in the 1800s due to efforts by missionaries to outlaw all spiritual practices of the people living on the islands,[33] ho'oponopono has made a comeback in recent years. Today it's a common means of solving family disputes in Hawaii, and many family law practices use it in mediation. In his article "Cutting the Cord: Ho'oponopono and Hawaiian Restorative Justice in the Criminal Law Context," Andrew J. Hosmanek explained the unique gifts ho'oponopono holds for people in conflict:

> Ho'oponopono is different from typical mediations because after the session is successfully completed, the participants figuratively cut the "cord" of legal and psychological entanglement that binds them; in other words, the dispute is put to rest forever. When victim and offender come to a true resolution of the problem, and jointly make the decision to move forward without further conflict on the issue, true healing can occur.[34]

The ancient wisdom of ho'oponopono is also being reignited to aid the youth of Hawaii who are in the state's judicial and foster care systems. One program, called Wahi Kana'aho, is run by Wayde Hoapili Lee, a Native Hawaiian cultural practitioner, and serves as a twenty-one-day residential program for kids who have gotten in trouble with the law or who are experiencing behavioral issues.[35] This program and others like it aim to build self-esteem and create a sense of belonging by reconnecting Hawaiians with their roots.

It is remarkable to see the same principles of equality, common purpose, and truth-telling in ancient Hawaii and other Pacific islands echoed in the Native American traditions of North America, as well as in the indigenous African values of *ubuntu*. These traditions of peacemaking were developed worlds away from one another in both time and space, yet carry very much the same intentionality.

Like these earth-based wisdom traditions and Buddhism, Coming to Peace embraces the understanding that peace can only happen when we recognize our connection to others and see the value of their experience as equal to our own. It can only happen when we look inward and try to understand our motivations and the effect these have on us and those around us. It can only happen when there is equality, respect, honesty, tolerance, compassion, and the taking of personal responsibility present in human interaction and conflict resolution. When these are present, we can heal disputes and return to a place of wholeness within ourselves and to the peace that is our essential nature.

CHAPTER 2: PEACE IN THE HEART OF CONFLICT

"If you can cultivate the right attitude, your enemies are your best spiritual teachers because their presence provides you with the opportunity to enhance and develop tolerance, patience and understanding."

- H.H. the Dalai Lama

After decades of working with individuals and groups, I have found that at our core we are fundamentally good and simply wish to be happy. I have also learned that our conflicts are just symptoms of larger issues going on within us and point to the ways in which we have twisted away from our true self. Once those issues are addressed, we will naturally realign with our essential nature. Coming to Peace is designed to help us reconnect with ourselves so that we may experience peace both inwardly and outwardly. To reach this goal, Coming to Peace offers a number of guiding principles to support the success of everyone in the process.

There truly is a wellspring of peace within each of us. To reach it, we must look in the most surprising place: right in the heart of conflict. When we examine our conflicts with others, a light shines on all the places where we have moved away from this wellspring. Conflict—and the path we must embark on to resolve it—serves as a beacon guiding us back to our inner peacefulness. To get there, we must first learn to recognize the kind of "light" or awareness that our conflicts with others are offering us.

Often it isn't until we've wandered far away from that place of inner peace and calmness that we encounter problems in our relationships with others. Through these disruptions, we are given the opportunity to gain awareness about the issues that are blocking access to our inner peace. By examining our struggles with others, we learn how conflict ultimately leads us back to this place of peace within ourselves.

However, this path is not an easy one. It is a radical practice to head toward our conflicts, rather than succumb to the urge to run away. But if we stay and do the work, we give ourselves the best chance we'll have at experiencing a lighter, more contented existence. If we stick with it, the Coming to Peace process will serve as a trusted guide on our journey to wholeness.

The first step of Coming to Peace is recognizing that conflict is a natural part of every relationship. Certainly we can all relate to experiencing disharmonies with family members, friends, or colleagues at one time or another; this is normal and to be expected. But if we've become trapped in a cycle of discontent with the people in our lives, then it might be time to examine the situation more closely.

Trouble most often begins when an imbalance of power occurs, leaving one person feeling overshadowed by the other. If one person's voice is continuously ignored in favor of another's, conflict inevitably arises. These types of power dynamics are at play in almost every group, including families, business organizations, and groups of friends. Within these groups there are natural hierarchies that emerge and alliances that form. The first and most influential group we experience is our family. Within family systems, power is usually concentrated in a small number of members, often one or both parents.

When conflict occurs in a group, such as a family, the first step toward resolution is the restoration of balance. The Coming to Peace process evens the playing field so that all members can feel empowered to give their account of the conflict. The process is based on the equality of all participants and requires everyone to voice their experience so they are heard by the group.

Being able to truly hear what someone is saying is a skill, especially if what the person is saying is something we don't want to hear. Listening in this way requires focus, intention, and the willingness to address any resistance that arises internally or within the group. Coming to Peace supports each person in this process of engaged listening by allowing only one person to speak at a time. This gives the speaker the space needed to share without being interrupted, and gives the others in the group the opportunity to hear what is being said.

When we're able to compassionately listen to each other, the larger picture begins to come into focus. This increases our ability to relate to the experiences of others in the group, experiences that we may not have been aware of or even considered. In this way, we begin to expand our self-awareness and understand how we impact the lives of others. This expanded awareness is vital for resolving conflict.

A basic tenet of Coming to Peace is the idea that everyone is our teacher. Friend, enemy, lover, sibling, child, parent—everyone in our life has something to teach us, particularly where conflict is involved. By examining how we respond to others, we discover what makes us tick, and what sets us off. Often, unbeknownst to us, we develop preferences over time that we employ in our relationships. These preferences include opinions or ideas that we have about others and ourselves. Although they're of our own creation, we deem them fact, and continue to engage and defend them at all costs. Despite the problems caused by pushing our preferences onto others, we often avoid looking more closely at the source of these preferences and their role in creating a cycle of discontent in our relationships.

Yet when we begin to explore these preferences, we start to see how our reactions to external events and the resulting conflicts are often a signal that something deeper is going on within us. Coming to Peace asks that we look honestly at our internal mental and emotional processes. While it might feel scary to look at these aspects of ourselves, doing so with a process such as

Coming to Peace allows us to begin to see ourselves through a more realistic lens.

The truth is, lack of clarity in motivation and intention—or the deliberate masking of negative motivation and intention—is the source of a lot of conflict.[1] To put it simply, intention informs motivation. So if we have a positive intention, we'll be motivated to act in a positive way. But if we have a negative intention, we'll be motivated to act negatively. Coming to Peace helps us recognize our intentions and motivations as well as those of others by insisting that everyone look honestly at themselves, tell the truth as they know it, and take responsibility for their intentions, motivations, and actions. When we engage in these practices, as well as self-reflection and the reflecting back of how others in the circle are experiencing us, some of the deepest teachings emerge. What begins to come into focus is the way in which we unwittingly create disharmony in our lives by pushing our personal agenda on others. The good news is that once we learn that we are hurting others, we can change our agenda so that it includes their wants and desires too. But we must dig deep to get to that point. While the demand for this level of authentic internal engagement requires a lot from us, Coming to Peace will be there to support us in our dedication to the restoration of peace.

As we will witness throughout the book, when each member of the group is genuinely participating in the process, the larger truth of the situation will emerge. To encourage and support this level of engagement, all participants are given the space needed to express themselves without fear of retribution or diminishment. Because everyone in the Coming to Peace circle shares equal power, no one can be scapegoated. It may take time for some, but once everyone finds the courage to share their experience honestly and to listen without prejudice, a new, larger truth begins to emerge, one that is informed by all the different experiences and nuances that have been feeding the conflict. It is from this larger truth and expanded vantage point that a path to resolution unfolds.

Still, it can be challenging to dismantle conflicts in social groups and families due to the various roles, structures, and hierarchies at play. With that said, avoiding them is not an option because members will remain locked in old ways of relating to each other, resulting in a continuous battle for leverage. Fortunately, Coming to Peace effectively disables these structures by giving all members the opportunity to share their side of the story, as well as the opportunity to reflect on the experiences of the others in the group. This takes time and patience, but offers lasting results.

While the process is valuable because it allows everyone to tell the truth of their experience regardless of their place on the proverbial totem pole, its effectiveness is greatly underscored when a member of the group refuses to take responsibility for their role in the conflict. As others honestly reflect their experience of the individual, the person's unwillingness to take responsibility becomes impossible to deny. In this way, the importance of taking personal responsibility is highlighted and on display for the entire group. This is an opportunity unlike any other because it effectively disrupts the constraints of the familial or social hierarchies that are usually in place, especially if the person refusing to take responsibility is at the top of the hierarchy.

In this way, unfair and unjust social and familial hierarchies simply cannot continue to function in the Coming to Peace process. As one teenager whose family participated in a Coming to Peace session said, "I felt for the first time that what I was seeing and saying was respected by the adults. They could not just say, 'That's it! Go to your room!' They had to stay and understand why they always want to cut me off when I am upset about being treated unfairly."

When it comes to Coming to Peace—and life, in general—the group cannot be in balance if even one of its members is out of balance. That is why the process places such a strong emphasis on truth and honesty, particularly within the individual. When each person is truthful about their experience and their role in a conflict, they help to bring balance to the group and themselves. This, in turn, brings them closer to resolution. But it can be a challenge to speak up to the group, and, at times, members may shy away from taking responsibility for their experience in the process, or it may take time to recognize how they may be contributing to the discord. When this occurs, they will be gently guided inward for a period of self-reflection. Self-reflection in the Coming to Peace process is supported by each person's connection to their inner wisdom and the understanding that our natural state is one of peace. This inner wisdom, which we will discuss in detail in Chapter 3, helps us reconnect with our essential nature, the *real* us, which is whole and not fragmented. The more we are able to connect with this state of wholeness, the happier we will be and the easier it will become to navigate any conflict that arises.

SECTION II

OUTER COMING TO PEACE

CHAPTER 3: BUILDING A FOUNDATION FOR PEACE

"Man must evolve for all human conflict a method which rejects revenge, aggression and retaliation. The foundation of such a method is love."

- Martin Luther King, Jr.

Every effective system requires a strong foundation to support the people within it so that they may succeed. The same is true for Coming to Peace. In this chapter, we'll discuss the core principles that guide the Coming to Peace process, the steps of the process, and the anatomy of a session. Understanding these important components will provide a clear view of what's to come. The foundation of Coming to Peace helps both the participants and the practitioner stay the course.

In order for Coming to Peace to help participants effectively resolve conflict, there are core principles that must be maintained. These principles include:

- Equality - Each person will be given equal time to speak, and every person's experience will be considered of equal value to the experience of every other member of the group.

- Mutual respect - Each person strives to treat other participants and the practitioner with respect. This means not interrupting someone when they are speaking and not making negative comments or characterizations.
- Honesty - Each person strives to tell the truth of their experience and be forthcoming about their actions.
- Commitment to personal responsibility - Each person remains fully accountable for their actions and agrees to seriously consider the effects those actions may have had on others.
- Compassion - Each person strives to hold a compassionate space for themself and the other members of the group.
- Tolerance - Each person agrees to practice tolerance even when they do not agree with what is being presented by other members of the group.
- Patience - Each person agrees to practice patience even when they feel upset by what is being presented by other members of the group.
- Willingness to engage - Each person agrees to participate in the process even when things become difficult, or when they do not like what is being brought forth in the session.
- Cultivation of inner wisdom - Each person agrees to do their best to attune to their inner wisdom by using the methods described below or by other practices they have studied.

In addition to these core principles, there are several additional elements to the Coming to Peace process that can help the group keep on task. Some of these are drawn from indigenous wisdom traditions, and offer simple, easily accessible ways for the group to stay focused and aligned throughout the reconciliation process.

Connecting to Inner Wisdom

Within each of us there is a place of inner wisdom or inner guidance. Throughout the Coming to Peace process participants are aided in connecting—or reconnecting—with their inner wisdom or inner guidance. To help members find this important voice within themselves, the practitioner leads a meditation. The inner wisdom may be seen or felt as a person, plant, animal, light, or any form that has meaning to the individual. It may also come through as a sound or sensation.

Like our fingerprints, our connection to this inner guidance is unique to each of us. Some people think of it as a connection to their higher self or some other aspect of the psyche. Others feel that a higher power from their spiritual tradition is what grounds them. And still others consider their inner wisdom to be a facet of their imagination. There is no right or wrong way to connect with this form of transcendent help. It is not a belief system; it is simply a place of peace within us.

The beauty of connecting to our inner wisdom is that once we discover this lifelong resource, we can check in with it whenever we're feeling disconnected, out of sorts, or pulled away from our positive intention. This internal compass will always point us back home; we just have to keep checking in with ourselves.

Setting Intention

At the outset of each Coming to Peace session, it's important that participants set an intention for the session. This can be an individual statement, with each person declaring an intention for the conflict resolution process. Or, it can be a group statement of intent, one that is said by each person in the group as a kind of promise or indicator of a shared purpose. For example, in a courtroom when a person swears to "tell the truth, the whole truth, and nothing but the truth," they are setting an intention for what they will say in the courtroom. These statements help clarify the purpose of the session for the individual and the group, as well as help everyone focus on the goal of peace. Here are sample statements of intention:

"My intention is to speak honestly about my experience without holding back because of fear."

"My intention is to better understand my anger and channel it in a productive way."

"My intention is to listen openly and without prejudice to what others have to say."

"My intention is to stay part of this process until I feel resolved."

By stating an intention, participants make it clear that they are committed to achieving peace. They also partake in a kind of ritual that joins them together in the process, similar to taking a vow or making a pledge. It's easy to overlook the importance of this, but on a subtle psychological level it's an offering that each person makes to themselves and to the group that helps them stick to their commitment. Also, the intention helps the practitioner understand what each person hopes to get out of the experience, and allows them to better guide and support participants throughout the entire process.

Setting Space

As we'll see in the client sessions throughout this book, the resolution process can become quite intense at times. To hold the variety of emotions that arise, the group must work together to generate and maintain a sturdy "container" or environment. Setting space helps create that container. It can be seen as a mindful holding of intention for the events that will take place in the space, as well as a clearing of the residue of past events. When setting space, the practitioner creates a neutral field and puts forth an intention of fairness and mutual respect that supports participants when they enter the mediation.

The setting of space has its roots in indigenous societies. In these cultures, the person assigned to manage the mediation session was also charged with setting and maintaining the space where the council was held. What this means is that the practitioner would clear the space of any imprints from prior activities that had occurred in the space so that an intention for its current use could be made and held. This would have been done through some sort of ritual, blessing, or prayer, and perhaps the lighting of incense, sage, or other herbs. For instance, the Iroquois would burn purifying herbs like sweet grass or sage prior to working in the space where the mediation was to be held.[1]

To some, the practice of setting space may seem archaic or ritualistic and not relevant to our contemporary society. But the truth is we engage in ritual all the time, often without knowing it. In some cases, the ritual has lost its meaning, so we don't infuse it with a conscious intention.

Today, Catholic priests, Buddhist monks, and other spiritual practitioners still light incense during ceremonies in order to clear the ceremonial space. Likewise, people who meditate or have a contemplative practice often light candles or incense for a similar purpose.

The idea of clearing a space of past imprints is also not that different from someone deciding to take a walk to "clear their head" after a stressful or heated experience. That conscious act helps break the chain of negativity that can continue to escalate without intervention. Though it may seem simple, setting space can have a profound effect on the session and everyone involved.

In a Coming to Peace session the practitioner sets the space. How this is done is up to the practitioner. Clearing a space may be as simple as opening a window to let in fresh air, or it may involve burning purifying herbs or incense. Lighting a candle or using an infuser with some aromatic oil is another way to cleanse a space before using it. What the practitioner chooses to use in setting a space will depend on personal preference and what they feel will best support the process.

Holding Space

The Coming to Peace practitioner actively cultivates the qualities of compassion and emotional neutrality necessary to navigate the sometimes rugged terrain of conflict resolution. They also actively generate a peaceful and grounded space for participants so that participants can make personal realizations about their particular role in the conflict. The practitioner first does this by having participants connect with their inner wisdom or inner guide at the beginning of each session. Then the practitioner holds a compassionate disposition and kindness of spirit in an effort to keep the collective in balance. If someone in the group loses focus and is putting their desires above others', the practitioner gently reminds them to consider how they are affecting the group.

The practitioner must model patience, honesty, and kindness toward the participants and the process itself. When the practitioner displays these qualities, participants will feel comfortable telling their truth, and will be more likely to treat themselves and others with the same kind of respect they are receiving from the practitioner and the group.

Finally, the practitioner is responsible for championing equanimity at all times. Equanimity is the view that all people and their experiences are of equal importance. This is fostered—with the help of the practitioner— through calm, nonjudgmental communication in all Coming to Peace sessions. As we will witness in the case studies in the following chapters, the desire to attain insight by learning what conflict has to teach us is an essential element of Coming to Peace. It is the role of the practitioner to nurture this attitude of inquiry and honesty and to help participants reach a collective understanding that allows for peaceful resolution.

Steps of Coming to Peace

The steps of Coming to Peace help everyone stay on the path to peace. They are designed to create equality among participants and give them the space and time needed to share their experience truthfully.

1. The participants and the practitioner sit in a circle.
2. The practitioner leads a guided meditation for connecting with inner wisdom.
3. Each person states their intention for participating in the process.
4. A "talking stick" or other object is passed around the circle to

indicate whose turn it is to speak. Upon receiving the stick, each person has the opportunity to speak or pass the stick. Only one person can speak at a time. There is no "cross talk" allowed.

5.   The practitioner manages the space and makes sure that participants remain respectful and adhere to the rules. The practitioner may also point to potential paths for the participants to explore to keep them on track.

6.   If an individual fails to maintain respect for others or themself, the practitioner asks them to take a break to reconnect with their inner guidance before reentering the conversation.

7.   The process continues until the stated time ends, typically one hour. If a resolution has not been reached, another session is scheduled for a later date.

8.   The practitioner may assign participants with a subject for further inner reflection to engage in between sessions.

The Process in Action

Once the practitioner has set the space and all the participants have stated their intention, the Coming to Peace session begins. At the outset of a session, the practitioner leads a guided meditation to help participants connect with their inner wisdom, or simply asks participants to silently connect with this place of guidance and truth within themselves. Once everyone makes this connection, they are asked to look at their own truth and their own understanding of the roots of the conflict.

The practitioner then begins the conversation by asking each person to share their experience of the situation and what they believe is the source of the conflict. They also are asked to state how they feel about the conflict. Everyone in the circle has equal access to the "floor." No one can interrupt or talk over another, including the practitioner. Everyone speaks successively until no one has anything left to say. During this progression, when it's the practitioner's turn to speak, they may offer a reflection, ask a question to be answered by each member of the group, or pass the talking stick. In this way, the practitioner is always encouraging participants to engage in honest self-examination to work toward a harmonious resolution.

The only time the practitioner would interrupt or speak out of turn is in the extraordinary instance that someone refused to relinquish the talking stick or was being abusive in some way.

As a rule, Coming to Peace requires that all members of a conflict have time to fully express their experience. A talking stick, or other object indicating whose turn it is to speak, gives everyone equal opportunity to express themselves. Taken from the resolution practices of the Iroquois and other traditional societies, the talking stick is passed from person to person. The only person who can speak is the one holding the stick. This ensures that no one is interrupted.[2] The passing of the stick is repeated as many times as needed for each person to speak their mind and respond to what others have said in the circle.

There are many advantages to using a talking stick or other object, not least of which is that it requires participants to consider their responses before speaking. It provides them numerous opportunities to practice patience and to resist speaking impulsively, allowing greater time for reflection. This is important because lack of patience and lack of spaciousness is one of the main reasons conflicts continue to spiral.

Some people may resist the process of inner reflection and the taking of personal responsibility. If they do not respect others in the circle or refuse to consider the welfare of others in the group, the practitioner guides them into a period of silence. This gives them the opportunity to reconnect with their inner guidance and reflect on what is required of them in order to maintain a harmonious connection within themselves and to the rest of the group.

On the surface, conflict is a disagreement between two or more individuals. However, underneath it's rarely that simple. Usually, conflict consists of many unconscious elements arising from the individuals involved, which is why it is so important to be willing to look honestly at our motivations and habitual reactions, and why a well held space is so important. Examining our troubles with others can yield positive results, but it can also be challenging at times. Participants may begin to feel fear and resistance as they approach the conflict resolution process. This is normal and to be expected. It's also why the practitioner must take great care when preparing the space, why the guidelines must be stated clearly, and why there is an emphasis on connecting to inner wisdom.

When a solid foundation is put in place, Coming to Peace serves as a strong, compassionate container that allows all participants to feel secure as they tell the truth of their experience. Throughout this book we will see the importance of upholding these practices, and how vital they are to supporting people wholly, as they come to peace with others and themselves.

CHAPTER 4: RESOLVING CONFLICT WITH OTHERS

"Peace between countries must rest on the solid foundation of love between individuals."

- Mahatma Gandhi

When we begin to dissect the conflicts in our lives, our education of how we treat others and ourselves commences. To say that this education may sting at times is an understatement. But it is on this necessary path through the heart of conflict that we find a place of true connection with others and balance within ourselves.

In this chapter, we will see, through case examples, how the Coming to Peace components of clarity of intention, personal responsibility, truth-telling, equality, respect, inner wisdom, and reflection work together to resolve conflict, and how a carefully prepared space holds the emotions of all participants so that everyone's voice may be heard. Here we will look at how the process of Coming to Peace works in solving problems between community members, family members, and couples. We will also be introduced to the Inner Coming to Peace process and gain insight into how it, too, contributes to the resolution of conflict.

Coming to Peace in Community

The term "community" implies togetherness, inclusiveness, and belonging for those who are members. In many ways, a community serves as an extended family. But in some cases what makes one person different can tear at the fabric of a community, fueling a fiery path of conflict all the way back to the person's family. That's what happened when George, a young gay man, came out to his family and their strict religious community.

Growing up in the heart of Georgia in a Southern Baptist household, George was anything but accepting of his budding homosexual feelings during adolescence. Always fearing ostracism by his church community and family, George faced many difficulties trying to find his way as a gay man in an unaccepting environment. When he finally found the strength to come out, his worst fears came true: Not only did his community shun him; so did his parents.

George's godfather, Michael, supported the young man fully. Determined to help reunite George with his parents and the larger community, Michael turned to the Coming to Peace process. He invited his nephew, Linda (George's mother), Peter (George's father), and members of the community to participate.

Even though George and his family were longstanding congregants of the church, no one from the community was interested in supporting George in this process. Even his own father refused, proclaiming that he "no longer had a son."

However, Linda agreed to participate because she loved her son dearly, even though she struggled with her belief that being gay was wrong. She also had difficulty separating from her husband's point of view on all manner of issues. Yet her participation in the Coming to Peace process with Michael and George led to the start of some very deep healing for them all.

At the beginning of the session, I led the participants in a meditation for inner wisdom or inner guidance. Linda found an angel as her guide, George's guide took the form of a wise man with a staff, and Michael discovered a white pearl that could reflect things from inside and outside. They found their source of inner guidance in a way that was individually meaningful to them. Each person had their own understanding of what help this guidance might offer.

(Note: Within all transcripts, I refer to myself as "Practitioner.")

Practitioner: *Please take a moment to connect with the inner guidance you have found. What are we here to work on today?*

Linda: *I want to understand why things went so wrong with my son. He was always a good boy and I don't understand how he could have turned out this way. He must have done something wrong to be gay. I must have done something wrong to have a gay son. His father must have done something bad to have a gay son. I am so lost and upset.*

George: *I want to be accepted for who I am. I want my mother to see that there's nothing wrong with me.*

Michael: *I want to help. That is all.*

Practitioner: *Could each of you say something in response to what the others have said?*

Linda: *I want to believe that there is nothing wrong with my son. He was always a good boy. But his father believes there is definitely something wrong with him.*

George: *I really think you need to think for yourself for once, Mom. How can Dad be right if you know I've always been a good boy?*

Michael: *I really feel like it is possible for understanding to come out of this. I support everyone here, but I don't think people should be made wrong for their choices.*

Linda: *I can't believe you can be gay, George. Did something happen to you? What did we do to deserve this? There must be something wrong with you.*

George: *I can't believe you could even wonder if there's something wrong with me for being gay.*

Michael: [Passes the talking stick]

Linda: *You must have done something wrong. I must have done something wrong.*

George: *Why? Why did something bad have to happen for me to be gay? I didn't do anything wrong and you didn't do anything wrong. I am just gay. I just like men.*

Michael: [Passes the talking stick]

Linda: *Don't say that! How could you say that?*

George: *Don't say what?*

Michael: [Passes the talking stick]

Linda: *Don't say that you like men!*

George: *Mom, cool it. You need to get that there's nothing wrong with being gay.*

Michael: [Passes the talking stick]

Linda: *Michael, say something! Tell him there's something wrong here!*

George: *There is nothing wrong here. There is nothing wrong with me, and there is nothing wrong with you, or Dad—except that he won't talk to me.*

Michael: *Linda, I have to agree with George. I don't think there is anything wrong with anyone, except that you and Peter cannot accept your son for who he is. I think in your heart you know that I'm right. You've always loved George and you've always supported everything he does. How could he suddenly be bad after all the good he has done? Think about how he always went to the food bank at Christmas and Thanksgiving to help out when he was in high school. That was his idea. No one told him he had to do that.*

Linda: [Crying] *Everything is for something. Nothing bad happens without a reason. Nothing is just circumstantial. If you are being punished, you must have done something wrong.*

George: *I disagree. Things just happen. Things just are. Besides, nothing bad is happening here. I am not being punished because I did something wrong by being gay. You are not being punished because you have a gay son. You did not do anything wrong.*

41

I did not do anything wrong. I just like men. You and Dad are the only ones doing any punishing "for no reason."

Michael: [Passes the talking stick]

Linda: *You have to stop saying that about men!*

George: *I am not going to stop saying it. You need to start hearing it. And you need to start hearing that Dad is just clueless. I didn't do anything wrong for him to reject me the way he is. I do not deserve to be punished, and I am not being punished because I am gay—except by him. And he is wrong, and you are wrong to say that there is something wrong with me because I'm gay.*

Michael: [Passes the talking stick]

Practitioner: *I think it would be helpful if everyone checked in with their inner guidance to see if bad things happen because people are being punished, or if things just happen—good or bad.*

[Silence]

Linda: *I am aware of all the times I thought other people were having a bad time because they had done something wrong.*

George: *Defining things as bad or good is just a definition.*

Michael: *Things just are.*

Linda: *I've been thinking that I must be a bad mother to have a gay son, but I know in my heart that I did my best to be a good mother. I keep thinking there's something I missed, but I can't think of what that might be.*

George: *Mom, you were a great mom. You are being a great mom now, coming here even though Dad didn't want you to. You have never done something he didn't want you to do. It's okay to break the rules and think for yourself.*

Michael: *And it is okay too for George to "break the rules" and think for himself.*

Linda: [Passes the talking stick]

George: *I used to think, that if I could just like girls, if I had just tried harder, it would be better. But it never got better. I just got unhappier. I don't want you to think you are a bad mom because I'm gay. There is nothing you could have done. Just like there's nothing that I could have done.*

Michael: *Things are as they are.*

Linda: *I'm confused. I know it's not good to think that other people are bad, but there has to be an explanation for why bad things happen.*

George: *Maybe the explanation is that I'm just gay.*

Michael: *As I said, things are as they are.*

Linda: *But I thought everything happens for a reason.*

George: *Maybe, maybe not.*

Michael: [Passes the talking stick]

Linda: *There must be something to blame. There must be someone to blame.*

George: *Well it's not me, and it's not you.*

Michael: *There is no one to blame.*

Linda: *I'm confused.*

George: *One thing I'm not confused about is that I love you.*

Michael: [Passes the talking stick]

Linda: [Crying] *It's just that this is so hard. Everyone thinks we did something wrong.*

George: *If you care about what everyone thinks, you'll never know who you are. That's one thing I've figured out over the last five years.*

Michael: *Who is "everyone?"*

Linda: *I don't know…Peter, the neighbors, the community, the whole church.*

George: *Mom, you're letting everyone and everything get in the way. You know who I am. I know who you are.*

Michael: [Passes the talking stick]

Linda: *I didn't know you were gay.*

George: *Come on, Mom. Come on.*

Michael: [Passes the talking stick]

Linda: [Crying] *I love you.*

George: *I love you too, Mom. There is nothing wrong here.*

Michael: *There is definitely nothing wrong here with George. There is something wrong with letting other people's opinions or ideas come between your love for your son, Linda.*

Linda: *I do love my son.*

George: *I know you do, Mom. I know you do.*

Michael: *I think you need to give him a chance to just be who he is.*

Linda: *What will Peter say?*

George: *Dad will come around, Mom. It doesn't matter what he says now. He'll change his mind when he sees that I can live a good life and be gay.*

Michael: [Passes the talking stick]

Linda: *But I have to live with him.*

George: *Or not... Sorry, Mom. I didn't mean that. But you have a right to make your own choices. I don't want you to have to choose between Dad and me. But I'm not dealing with Dad right now. I'm dealing with you. And it's important to me that you get that nothing bad is happening here. It is okay that I'm gay. No matter what anyone says. I have fought long and hard to say that out loud. And I know it's true.*

Michael: *I think you have to do and think what is right for you, Linda. Just right now, think about how much you love your son.*

Linda: *Yes, I have to think about that.*

George: *Okay. Good. And try and think there is nothing wrong with me...and nothing wrong with you. Okay?*

Michael: [Passes the talking stick]

Linda: *Okay.*

Practitioner: *Okay, this will end the session for today. It sounds like the theme to contemplate for further work is the importance of love.*

During their Coming to Peace sessions, Linda and George were able to move past the judgments of the community and meet each other where their relationship had begun, at a place of deep love for one another. Because Coming to Peace requires that only one person speak at a time, their tradition of wounding each other during arguments where everyone talked and no one listened was quickly terminated. As a result, Linda was able to open up and connect with her son again, and George, after many years of overwhelming self-doubt, was relieved to have a forum within which he could advocate for himself without interruption.

George finally found his voice and was able to challenge his mother and her rigid belief system. He learned that to free himself from the conflict, he had to cease muting his nature in order to pacify her. By learning to put his own truth before the values of others, George was able to free himself from his own internal conflicts surrounding his sexuality.

For Linda, the Coming to Peace circle provided a safe and neutral space where she could evaluate her beliefs and how they were fueling the painful conflict that threatened to end her relationship with her son. She was able to see more clearly how her narrow belief system of "good" and "bad" was not only limiting her experience of life, but was so strong that it almost separated her from the love she felt for her child. Linda vowed to put her connection with her son first and her belief system second, even as she continued to examine her way of viewing the world, and deal with her husband's sustained disapproval.

Both Linda and George were lucky to have Michael's influence and support. He understood that conflict could only persist in the family if a blind adherence to an inflexible belief system that alienates its members took precedence over their love for each other. The processes of Coming to Peace created the breathing room necessary for that truth to come to light, and laid the foundation for further understanding of the conflict to emerge.

Coming to Peace in Families

Family systems can create an environment that fosters conflict, especially when its members are expected to remain loyal to parents or other members who hold all the power. For this and many other reasons, family members can trigger each other without even knowing how or why. That was the case with a struggling family of five who came to see me for help.

Veronica (mother), Joel (stepfather), and their three daughters: Erica (15), Ashley (13), and Megan (8) were in a state of despair when they entered their first Coming to Peace session. The entire family was suffering from the volatile relationship between Joel and Ashley. It had gotten so bad between the two that they were unable to successfully sit down to work things out without one or both of them resorting to angry outbursts.

First, I led all of the participants in the meditation for inner guidance. Veronica found a blue dove whose primary characteristic was that it was very peaceful. Joel found a yellow column of light whose primary characteristic was that it was compelling. Erica found a large giraffe that was very calm. Ashley found a Tweety Bird-like character whose primary characteristic was that it was funny. Megan found a unicorn with a purple mane that liked to play, and made her feel safe.

Again, everyone found this source of inner guidance in their own way and in a way that had individual meaning to each of them. There was no effort to "standardize" the experience of truth. Each person felt their own sense of what this guidance had to offer.

Practitioner: *Let's take a moment to focus inward and connect with the inner guidance you have just encountered. What are we here to work on today?*

Veronica: *I am here because my heart is broken because the people I love hurt each other and me.*

Joel: *I am here because we are having a problem with anger. I am having a problem with anger.*

Erica: *I'm here because I was told I had to be here.*

Ashley: *I'm here because he [Joel] is a jerk.*

Megan: *Mom and Dad brought me here.*

Practitioner: *Can everyone offer a response to the reasons everyone has mentioned for being here?*

Veronica: *I agree there is a problem with anger. I'm glad Erica agreed to be here, and that Megan is here too. I'm hoping Ashley can begin to see her stepfather in a new way.*

Joel: *I'm sorry to hear that this anger is causing so much heartache for Veronica. And I appreciate Erica and Megan being here. I want to find a new way to talk to Ashley so that she doesn't think I'm a jerk.*

Erica: *I'm hoping this helps Mom. I'm tired of hearing Ashley always talk trash about Joel. I want something to change.*

Ashley: *I don't care what Erica wants. I don't care how Mom feels. I have to deal with this jerk all the time, and no one cares.*

Megan: [Passes the talking stick]

Veronica: *We do care about everyone, and that's why we're here.*

Joel: *What makes you think I'm a jerk?*

Erica: [Passes the talking stick]

Ashley: *You always tell me what to do. You used to be really nice when you were coaching the softball team. Now, it's "you didn't do that right, you didn't do this right." You aren't my father—who are you to tell me what I'm doing right and what I'm doing wrong?*

Megan: [Passes the talking stick]

Veronica: [Passes the talking stick]

Joel: *I'm just trying to help you learn the game. I'm just trying to help.*

Erica: [Passes the talking stick]

Ashley: *You don't help anything. You're always in my face, yelling at me and telling me what to do.*

Megan: [Passes the talking stick]

Veronica: [Passes the talking stick]

Joel: *I'm just trying to help you learn. I know I get frustrated sometimes when I feel like you aren't listening. I'm just trying to help fill in for your dad.*

Erica: *I don't think it's possible to fill in for Dad.*

Ashley: *You are not my dad!*

Veronica: *Why don't you think it's possible to fill in for Dad?*

Megan: [Passes the talking stick]

Joel: *Yes, I would like to know that as well.*

Erica: *Because Dad's a loser. He never shows up. He never does anything. He always says he's going to do something, and then he doesn't. There's no making up for that. Only he can make up for that, and he never does.*

Ashley: [Crying]

Megan: [Passes the talking stick]

Veronica: *I don't know what to do.*

Joel: *I know he doesn't show up. That's why I try to show up double time. I am trying to help fix that problem, but maybe my trying to make everything right is the wrong thing.*

Erica: *No, you really can't make it right—only he can.*

Ashley: *I didn't know you were trying to make things right for us because Dad doesn't show up. It just seems like you're always around and not giving me any space to make my own choices.*

Megan: [Passes the talking stick]

Veronica: [Passes the talking stick]

Joel: *I'm sorry I'm not giving you space. I worry that you're going to feel bad when your dad says he's going to show up and he doesn't. I am sorry I yell at you when you're not getting what I'm trying to show you. I think I must be mad at him...and I'm yelling at you. I'm trying to protect you from the loss of him, but I'm not doing a very good job.*

Erica: *Thanks for trying.*

Ashley: *I didn't know you were mad at Dad. I think I'm mad at him too.*

Megan: [Passes the talking stick]

Veronica: *It seems like you are both mad at Dad and taking it out on each other.*

Joel: *I am so sorry. I will really work on this. I think I've been mad at myself too because I can't make everything right for you guys. And I think I've been taking that anger out on you. I am really sorry.*

Erica: *That sounds right.*

Ashley: *I think it sucks that Dad doesn't show up.*

Megan: [Passes the talking stick]

Veronica: *I know it's hard.*

Joel: *Let's work on this between us, and try to make our family happier.*

Erica: *I think we should talk to Dad about the way he doesn't show up for us.*

Ashley: *I'm sorry I called you a jerk.*

Practitioner: *It's good that you are seeing the deeper reason for this conflict, and it's important to recognize the similarities between your individual experiences. It would be helpful to reflect on this point going forward.*

Utilizing the Coming to Peace guidelines of equality and speaking one at a time, each member was able to voice their experience of the conflict to the other members of the family. As a result, Joel and Ashley were able to truly hear each other; and they began to recognize their part in the disharmony and the effect it was having on the whole family.

One unexpected development arose during the process. As the family delved into the details of the conflict, it became clear that the behavior of Ashley, Megan, and Erica's biological father, Rob, was having a negative effect on all of them. Rob did not participate in the Coming to Peace sessions. In fact, it was his inability to "show up" as a parent that caused everyone in the family pain. To mitigate Rob's general absence in the girls' lives, Joel had decided to step into the father role and be the best dad he could be for his stepdaughters. Yet his desire to make things better for them made him overbearing in ways he hadn't realized, and this is what led to the ongoing conflict with Ashley. Specifically, he pushed her to excel at school and sports, and became frustrated with her when she could not understand something he was trying to explain to her. His zeal for being a good dad made him lose sight of the true objective: loving and supporting Ashley.

For her part, Ashley hadn't realized that Joel was actually trying to make up for her father's irresponsibility by being a better father to her. This was revelatory. Her anger with him was, in part, justified because of the way he pushed her. But when she realized it was out of love, not disapproval, her hostility toward her stepfather changed. In the open environment of Coming to Peace, Ashley and Joel were able to see each other from a fresh perspective. This caused Joel to pull back on his overbearingness and Ashley to appreciate him for his desire to be a good dad. They also were able to see exactly how much damage their fiery engagements were having on the rest of the family, which helped them to stop yelling and start listening, and gave them the strength to open their hearts to each other and the other family members.

After tracing their angry and hurt feelings back to the source, the process of a genuine reconciliation of forgiveness between Ashley and Joel began. As they took responsibility for the way in which they had both been contributing to the unhappiness of the other family members and each other, peace returned to them all. And as a unit, the family made the decision to address the girls' father in a direct and honest way regarding his lack of integrity. They also promised to continue communicating clearly and honestly with each other.

Coming to Peace with Couples

When we enter into a union with another person, it's difficult to foresee in this early stage of our relationship the kinds of problems that might arise down the line. When the going gets tough, we sometimes find ourselves unprepared to handle conflict with our partner. That's what happened to Sarah and John, a couple who arrived at my office to address problems in the relationship that revolved around John's inability to secure a new job after losing his to an industry shift that made his profession obsolete. Further complicating matters, Sarah had stopped working years earlier due to an illness, and, though she had recovered, she had not returned to work.

The following Coming to Peace sessions occurred between the couple. Sarah's inner guidance presented itself as a large willow tree whose primary characteristic was that it was serene. And John's guide was a big sea turtle that he experienced as being strong and steady.

Session 1

Practitioner: *Let's take a moment to focus inward and connect with the inner guidance you have just encountered. What are we here to work on today?*

Sarah: *I am here because I want John to get it that he needs to get another job quick.*

John: *I am here because I need help figuring out what to do about my job and our finances. I'm getting older, and I'm afraid I'm not going to be able to get another job.*

Practitioner: *Can each of you offer a response to the reasons the other has mentioned for being here?*

Sarah: *He is always so pessimistic. He needs to get another job.*

John: *I don't know why she is so angry. I am just trying to solve a problem. But I'm not doing a very good job at it.*

Sarah: *Well, that's typical. If you had been doing a better job at work, you wouldn't be losing your job.*

John: *I do my best. The industry is changing, and the technology that I manage is becoming obsolete. That's not something I can control.*

Sarah: *You should be able to figure out how to stay up to date. How are you going to keep any job if you don't?*

John: *I try to keep my skills updated, but things change so fast.*

Practitioner: *Can each of you say how well you think you are taking personal responsibility, and how well you think the other person is taking personal responsibility?*

Sarah to the practitioner: *I don't like your tone.*

John: *I feel like I'm not doing enough to make things better. I don't know how Sarah is taking personal responsibility here.*

Practitioner: *I'm sorry you did not like my tone. Let me repeat the question: Can each of you say how well you think you are taking personal responsibility and how well you think the other person is taking personal responsibility?*

Sarah: *What kind of a question is that? What do you mean, "taking personal responsibility?" What does that mean?*

John: *I think it means, "What is everyone doing to try and solve the problem in a responsible way?"*

Sarah: *Well, this is not my problem to solve. If you were staying up to date with your skills, we wouldn't have a problem.*

John: [Eyes welling with tears] *I don't know what to do.*

Practitioner: *Can you each take a moment to connect with your inner guidance to see what insights it might offer about personal responsibility?*

[Silence]

Sarah to the practitioner: *This is really a bunch of hooey. I thought you were going to do your job and get him where he needs to be with getting up to speed with the job market.*

John: *When I connect with my inner guidance, I feel like there really isn't anything else I should be doing to take responsibility. In fact, it seems like I may be taking too much responsibility. But I'm not really sure what that means.*

Practitioner: *I think it would be helpful, Sarah, if you took a moment to reflect on your last statement, and see how what you said reflects or does not reflect respect for everyone here.*

Sarah: *Jesus!*

[Silence]

John: *I don't understand why it's only my responsibility to have a job. You could get a job. Why is this only my problem?*

Sarah: *Great. Now you want me to go back to work and get sick again. Great.*

John: *You've been well for several years now. I think you can find a job that doesn't tire you out the way your old one did.*

Sarah: *We are talking about you and your job. This is your problem. This is not my problem. I can't work. If I work, I'll get sick again. Now you're trying to make me work. Great. Just great. You're a great provider!*

John: [Sits in silence]

Practitioner: *I think it would be helpful, Sarah, if you took a moment to reflect on your last statement, and how what you said reflects or does not reflect respect for everyone here.*

[Silence]

Sarah: *I am not going back to work, and that is final.*

John: *I'm not sure this is going anywhere positive.*

Sarah: *Well, at least we agree on something!*

Practitioner: *It might be helpful for you both to reflect on your relationship to personal responsibility. In particular, it would be helpful if you can think about how you take responsibility and what you take responsibility for.*

Session 2

Practitioner: *Let's just take a moment of silence and connect to inner guidance.* [Silence] *So, do you have any insights about responsibility, or is there anything else you would like to talk about today?*

John: *Well, I've been thinking about something that happened at my old job that I want to talk about. The whole network for the printer system had gone down because my boss tried to jerry-rig a fix for another part of the network. When I came in on my day off to work on it, he just yelled at me and told me it was my fault. That was not true. He was the one who made the problem happen. When he was yelling at me, I felt like a kid. I felt so powerless, and then I started blaming myself, even though I knew it was his fault. But I felt better when I started blaming myself. It seemed like something was wrong with that, because it was his fault. Why did I feel better when I was blaming myself?*

Sarah: *You got me. I don't really have a lot to say.*

Practitioner: *So, John, why do you think you were feeling better when you were blaming yourself?*

John: *It seems like blaming myself is better than feeling powerless.*

Sarah: [Passes the talking stick]

Practitioner: *What is it like to see that you feel better being blamed than feeling like you are powerless?*

John: *I think this is why the job thing has been so hard, because I feel powerless to change anything. I don't like feeling powerless. It seems like I would rather feel anything except powerless. I would even rather take blame for something I'm not responsible for than feel powerless.*

Sarah: *Well, you are to blame for a lot of stuff.*

John: *I realize I blame myself for a lot of stuff I'm not to blame for. And I think you blame me for a lot of stuff I'm not to blame for. When my boss was yelling at me, it felt the same as that time when you were yelling at me because you locked the keys in the car.*

Sarah: *Well, if you hadn't left the bags in the car, I wouldn't have had to go back and get them, and I wouldn't have locked the keys in the car.*

John: *I really think I let you blame me for a lot of stuff because I'd rather be wrong than powerless. Powerless is just the worst thing. But I feel like I can't get any traction to get a new job because I'm yelling at myself for losing this job. But it isn't my fault that the technology is changing; the whole industry is going to disappear. That cannot be all my fault.*

Sarah: *Well, I'm feeling pretty powerless at getting you to get a grip and get another job.*

Practitioner: *It seems like it would be helpful if you could both reflect for a moment on what it means to be powerless.*

John: *I really see that I avoid being powerless at all costs. But I cannot avoid it in this situation. I am powerless about the whole industry changing. I can't avoid it. I see that I've been letting you blame me for stuff around the job so that I wouldn't feel this powerlessness. I really need to think about this.*

Sarah: *If you would just get a job, I wouldn't feel powerless.*

John: *I think I need some time to myself to think about this.*

Practitioner: *It seems like it would be helpful if you could both reflect on the issues of powerlessness more in depth before the next session.*

In sessions with John and Sarah, the Coming to Peace qualities of truth-telling, inner-wisdom, and the importance of self-responsibility were on full display. Sarah made no bones about blaming John for having trouble finding a job. She wanted him to be the "provider," and she was unwilling to return to work out of fear that she would become sick again. As the mediation sessions progressed, it was evident that Sarah was not willing to look at how she was contributing to the problem. She blamed John and refused to examine her fear of returning to work as contributing to the couple's dynamic. Sarah's attitude in the sessions progressively became more negative as she avoided every opportunity to take responsibility for her part in the conflict. Ultimately, her behavior in the sessions helped John to see the way that he was inappropriately taking responsibility for the issues in their relationship. This also led him to the realization that he had been doing the same thing with his former boss.

Sarah became increasingly frustrated with the Coming to Peace process when it did not produce the results she had expected—to force John to find a job—and she decided to drop out for a time. John remained committed and went further to examine his struggles with others and himself. It was through his work with the Inner Coming to Peace process that John learned some life-changing information about himself.

Inner Coming to Peace refers to the processes of Coming to Peace that can be applied to our internal conflicts. These processes support people as they look more deeply at their motivations and behavior as a result of an external conflict. It helps illuminate hidden attitudes and unresolved emotional states that might be causing disharmony without us realizing it, and provides a way of integrating these internal conflicts so that they are no longer contributing to conflict in our life. We will discuss Inner Coming to Peace in greater depth in Chapter 6.

Through his personal work with Inner Coming to Peace, John discovered that he had been struggling with a deep-seated issue of self-blame and powerlessness both in his marriage and in the job he had recently lost. He realized how he had allowed himself to become a scapegoat in both areas of his life to try to avoid feeling the sense of powerlessness that arose whenever he was unable to meet the ever-increasing expectations of his frantic boss, who had been clinging to a failing business, and his wife, who wanted to avoid going back to work. Ultimately, John recognized that he needed to change his relationship with his wife. He decided to take a break from the marriage and move out to get some clarity on the nature of his way of relating to his wife and himself.

In the end, John was able to attain a level of peace he had not had before by looking honestly at his relationship to powerlessness. He stopped accepting blame inappropriately, and, as a result, came into greater balance within himself. After seeing John's success with Inner Coming to Peace, Sarah decided to do her own work and resumed addressing the issues in the marriage. Eventually, John and Sarah got back together and continued the work of Coming to Peace. John maintained a healthy boundary to taking on responsibility that was not his, and Sarah made great progress working on her own issues and was even able to go back to work. They are still together today.

The supportive environment of Coming to Peace helped the people discussed in this chapter reach a deeper understanding of what was causing their conflict. While John's experience so poignantly demonstrates the peace that is possible for each of us when we are willing to look inward at our own issues, all of the examples in this chapter shed light on how our inner conflicts can contribute to our external conflicts with others. It is in this way that Coming to Peace acts as a window into our sometimes hidden motivations, allowing us to see more clearly the elements feeding conflict. Only when we are willing to enter the heart of conflict and look more deeply within ourselves can we find understanding. And, as we will soon see, that is what the Inner Coming to Peace process is all about.

SECTION III

INNER COMING TO PEACE

CHAPTER 5: UNDERSTANDING THE SELF

"Men can starve from a lack of self-realization as much as they can from a lack of bread."

- Richard Wright

The unexamined self can be quite a fragile thing. There are many ways we can feel wounded by our circumstances. When we pull away from the pain of that wounding rather than try to approach and understand it, we lose track of the way it affects us. We can overreact to what is happening in a current situation as a result of our unexamined experience and this will often lead to conflict. By now we know that it is through examining this discomfort that we're able to gain a lifetime of insight. We just need to be willing to pull out the magnifying glass and take a closer look at our "self."

The "self" refers to our psyche. It's the lens through which we view and then experience the world. As you can imagine, inspecting the psyche, especially our own, is a complex undertaking. But if we refuse to do so, and continue to allow our internal conflicts to live a life outside of our awareness, we will continue to struggle to achieve true and lasting happiness. Because our unexamined intentions, motives, and unexpressed wounds feed the conflicts in our life, it's difficult, if not entirely impossible, to have a happy and balanced life if we don't make every effort to become aware of our entire experience, including the parts within us that we prefer to ignore.

When the methods of Coming to Peace are applied internally, we become more deeply aware of the workings of our psyche and learn to better discern which part of the conflict comes from within and which part does not. This helps us determine where our responsibility lies in the resolution process. But for this level of understanding to occur, we must first have an important conversation, not with another person, as we saw in the mediation sessions of the last chapter, but between the conflicting parts of the self.

The idea that different parts of the self exist and are shaping our experience has been around for a long time. Most famously, in 1920, Sigmund Freud revealed to the world his theory of the human psyche and its different parts—id, superego, and ego—in his groundbreaking article "Beyond the Pleasure Principle." He discussed the now well-known multi-part self model more in depth in his book *The Ego and the Id*.[1] To put it simply, according to Freud's model of the psyche, the id is the part of the self run by instinct, the superego is the moral or critical inner voice, and the ego is the part that tries to keep the peace between the id and superego.

While Freud's theory helps us begin to grasp the idea of the existence of different parts of the self and the disagreement that often occurs between them, it can be a bit "one size fits all" in its execution. In the Coming to Peace process and the self-examination that arises from trying to resolve an external conflict, we see not only the different parts of the self emerge, but also the myriad of expressions of each part in response to the person's experiences. In other words, how the parts of the self are expressed is unique to each of us—an idea that is not found in Freud's theory.

A much older theory of personality stems from a wisdom system that has been adopted by the spiritual traditions of Hawaii. In this system, the basis for understanding the nature of the self lies in the recognition of three spirits who come together to evolve and learn in one physical body. One is a spirit of physical processes, one is a spirit of mental and emotional processes, and the third is a spirit of higher wisdom that guides the first two toward ideal circumstances. According to this system, conflicts between the spirits are the basis for psychological disorder and physical disease. When a person is healthy physically, mentally, and emotionally, it is believed that they are well because of the harmony occurring between the three spirits or parts of the self.[2] If we consider these three spirits from a more contemporary viewpoint, as aspects of the psyche, they are noticeably similar to Freud's theory of personality involving the id, ego, and superego.

At first it may feel uncomfortable to recognize that there are different "voices" within us; we may worry that others will think we're mentally unbalanced. But there is no reason to be concerned, because it is completely normal to have different parts of the self with different views of the same experience.[3] In fact, Italian psychologist Roberto Assagioli's theory of personality called Psychosynthesis celebrates these various parts of the self or "subpersonalities," as he refers to them. In Assagioli's words, "Subpersonalities exist at various levels of organization, complexity, and refinement…" throughout the mind.[4] These subpersonalities drive decision-making in relation to others and the larger environment. According to Psychosynthesis, success in relationships, and in life in general, depends on the development and integration of these parts of the self.[5] If they are in conflict, we will remain in conflict with others. If they are in harmony, we will experience harmony in our relationships.

If we look closely, multiple parts of the self and their conflicting views and intentions are at play even in the most common experiences. For instance, say someone we will call Christine is about to start a new job, and there is a part of her that is anxious to prove herself and a part that is afraid to fail. The way the two parts of Christine relate differently to the job opportunity creates a potential internal conflict.

Trouble could arise if Christine's internal conflict is triggered. For example, if Christine's desire to prove herself were to cause her to become exhausted from working too hard, this could cause her to miss work or even miss deadlines. By overworking, she may actually do a subpar job. Then, her fear of failing would be realized and she could find herself in trouble with her boss or other colleagues.

One major benefit of Coming to Peace is the opportunity it gives us to gain clarity about our motivations. When we get locked into a conflict with another, the process encourages us to look inward and define our intentions in order to reach a resolution. By doing so, we gain awareness about what is driving us to act in certain ways. More often than not, the motivating factor is the result of an earlier experience, and, consequently, we are unwittingly reacting in old ways to new circumstances. For example, if Christine were to engage in the process and look at her motivations, she might discover the circumstances surrounding why one part of her fears the challenge of starting a new job, while another part looks forward to it. Then, she would have the opportunity to change her relationship to her experience on the job.

Joel

Another example of how the psyche can develop multiple parts with differing reactions to an external experience is found in the case of Joel, the overzealous stepfather from Chapter 4. If we recall, Joel identified his ongoing issue with anger, which kept showing up in interactions with his stepdaughter, Ashley. During the Outer Coming to Peace sessions, Ashley and Joel realized the actual cause of their frustration with each other was their shared anger at Ashley's father, not each other, and they were able to resolve their conflict and repair their relationship.

However, Joel's wish to improve his relationship with Ashley drove him to want to learn more about his inner process and how it might have been prompting the contentious interactions between them. Using Inner Coming to Peace methods, Joel explored his relationship with anger further. In these sessions, he uncovered a split within himself related to the way he took on responsibility. One part of him sought out responsibility, and the other part was angry at having to take on responsibility.

The following example is of one of Joel's Inner Coming to Peace sessions. It demonstrates how working with split parts of the self is similar to working with individuals in the Outer Coming to Peace process.

I used guided meditation to help Joel connect with his inner wisdom. Once Joel connected with his guide, a yellow column of light, he continued the meditation to identify the two parts of himself that were at odds over responsibility. Joel identified one part as a soldier that is located in the back of his head and another as a red ball in his stomach.

Practitioner: *I'd like you each to state your position on responsibility.*

Soldier: *It is important to take responsibility. You have to do your duty. You have to protect the weak.*

Red Ball: *I am sick of responsibility. Give me a break.*

Practitioner: *And how do you each respond to the other's position regarding responsibility?*

Soldier: *You are irresponsible. You don't have what it takes.*

Red Ball: *You are just a jerk Boy Scout. Every damsel in distress that comes your way tools you around.*

Practitioner: *Joel, can you ask what the Guide has to say about this situation?*

Guide: *I think it would be helpful if you both thought for a moment about the effect your words are having on each other.*

[Silence, during which both parts take a "time-out."]

Red Ball: *Okay. I'm sorry. I just think you don't consider what you're doing. You just rush into the burning house without thinking about how the fire got started.*

Soldier: *You have to take care of the problem. You can think about how it got started later.*

Red Ball: *I disagree. You need to think about how things happen. You just rush in, and you always get burned.*

Soldier: *It doesn't matter what happens to me.*

Red Ball: *Uh, yeah, it does, because what happens to you happens to me.*

Soldier: *What are you talking about?*

Red Ball: *You are so busy going around saving every cat up a tree that you don't think about taking care of us. You are overweight, you're still smoking, and you don't exercise. How do you think that affects me when I am trying to take responsibility for our health? You think I don't take responsibility? You need to look twice, buddy.*

Soldier: *Oh.*

Red Ball: *Yeah, "oh."*

[Silence]

Soldier: *Okay, I see what you mean. But I have to make things better. I have to protect the weak.*

Red Ball: *If I hear that one more time, I am going to puke. Protect the weak? Think about protecting us.*

Soldier: *Oh.*

Red Ball: *Yeah, "oh."*

[Silence]

Soldier: *I think I just don't know how to stop smoking, and whenever I try, you are not cooperating.*

Red Ball: *That might be true. I think I don't cooperate with you on anything because all your schemes are so stupid. I don't even pay attention to what you want anymore. I think that is true. I have to admit that.*

Soldier: *Well, maybe you need to listen to me sometimes.*

Red Ball: *Well, maybe you need to listen to ME sometimes.*

Soldier: *Okay.*

Red Ball: *Well, okay. And do me a favor: take a look at why you always have to save everyone except yourself.*

This was a truly eye-opening session for Joel. He discovered that one part of him was driven to help people, which manifested as him taking responsibility, often inappropriately, for their wellbeing. The other part of him was angry and rebelled at Joel's drive to take responsibility for others at the expense of his own health. This led to a destructive internal dynamic of one part trying to accomplish something and the other part resisting.

The session also revealed another habit Joel had of becoming forceful with those who refused to cooperate with him, such as with his stepdaughter, when he was trying to overcome the cynical voice of Red Ball. Joel realized that he expected the person he was trying to help to resist his efforts because he experienced that resistance within himself from Red Ball. To compensate, he became pushy with others in an unconscious attempt to override Red Ball's defiant response to Soldier's need to seek out responsibility. This projection of his expectation of resistance onto people caused Joel a lot of problems. He resolved to watch this behavior and to pay attention to what he needed to do to take better care of his health. Joel felt hopeful that taking both of these steps would lead to greater peace, both in his relationship with Ashley and himself.

By looking into the roots of his anger, Joel learned more about his role in creating conflict within his family, as well as what was fueling his anger and the steps he needed to take to reduce it. He also began exploring his need to compulsively help people. He hadn't realized that this impulse was causing an imbalance in him and that there may be more to explore in order to fully understand his drive to take responsibility for others.

Through the process of internal inquiry, we can mend the troubled relationship we have with ourselves and others. The internal mediation and integration processes of Coming to Peace are crucial for restoring harmony both externally and within the self. In the following chapters, we will learn more about the methods of Inner Coming to Peace and see more examples of how people have worked with them to resolve their hidden inner turmoil.

CHAPTER 6: FACING THE CONFLICT WITHIN

"He who knows others is wise; he who knows himself is enlightened."

- Lao Tzu

Once our eyes are open to the effects that internal battles have on relationships and how we experience life, we can begin to make changes with more ease and efficacy than was possible before. The sky is the limit when it comes to how far we want to go on this journey through conflict to gain a better understanding of ourselves and our evolution. By choosing to address these inner issues, we are moving toward creating the kind of lasting change needed for true happiness.

In the previous chapter we learned that to get to the source of our conflicts with others, we must become aware of any parts inside ourselves that are at odds. As with Outer Coming to Peace for couples and groups, Inner Coming to Peace provides the secure space and container needed for the conflicting parts of the self to come forward and tell the truth of their experience of the conflict. Admittedly, the idea of having multiple parts of the self expressing different opinions about a conflict is a lot to grasp at first, but as we delve more deeply into the process of Inner Coming to Peace, it will become clear how common this is, and how giving the parts the opportunity to converse and reconcile effects real change in the person's life.

As we saw in the Inner Coming to Peace session with Joel in Chapter 5, the once easily frustrated stepfather was able to reach an understanding about his anger and reconcile this not only with his stepdaughter, but also with himself. Apparent in the case of Joel as well as every other person in this book, the heart of the Coming to Peace reconciliation process lies in the connection between the individual and their inner wisdom. This is even more pronounced in the Inner Coming to Peace process, when inner guidance takes on a leading role.

How Inner Coming to Peace Works

Using guided mediation, the practitioner helps the participant relax into a lightly altered state, which allows them to connect with their guide—the part of the person that helps them access and support the conflicting parts within them. The importance of the guide cannot be stressed enough because it is the part of the person that is doing the largest share of the work. It is not an outside force, teacher, or therapist. It is a wise part of the self that is capable of seeing the entire picture and holding a compassionate space. Most people find this realization empowering. In fact, engaging this aspect of the self can give us confidence in our ability to navigate difficult situations, as well as provide us with a source of power from within that we can attune to whenever we're having a hard time.

Once the participant makes a connection with their inner guidance, the practitioner helps the participant bring forward the parts of the self that are driving the conflict. To begin, the participant identifies each part by locating its presence in the body. Then the practitioner asks the participant to perceive a form for each part. This helps differentiate between the parts and allows each one to relate its experience of the conflict and the conditions leading up to it. It's important to remember that these opposing parts are expressions of different points of view the individual holds. Giving each part a name or visual description not only helps differentiate between the parts, it can also shed a light on the perspective of each part. In addition to making these parts of the self more relatable, identifying them by their characteristics also highlights the dynamic the parts are creating with their differing views. How the parts identify themselves and the agendas they offer up often provides surprising clarity to the problem.

The thought of moving inward to reveal and name these parts of the self may seem awkward or even impossible at first. After all, the conscious mind is trained to resist the idea that other parts of the self even exist, let alone have the agency to affect our lives. This is precisely why an altered state is used in the process of Inner Coming to Peace—which is achieved through a guided meditation. It is in this state that we are able to loosen the grip of the conscious mind and its tendency to focus externally rather than on our internal experience. We are still fully aware of what we are saying and doing, but our minds are more relaxed and open to greater perception. From this expanded viewpoint, we are able to mend rifts created by the feuding parts of the self and their opposing agendas. This leads to authentic and long-lasting relief, and brings hope and new possibilities for untangling the resulting external conflicts.

Jonathan

Jonathan, a brilliant computer scientist, came to me for help because he could not establish a long-term relationship with a woman, despite his wish to be married and have a family. Every time he became involved with a woman, Jonathan lost interest after the third or fourth date. He attempted to date all types of women to increase his odds of finding love, but he continued to struggle with maintaining an interest in a woman.

By inspecting his romantic relationships for clues about why he was unable to enter into an intimate relationship despite his desire to do so, Jonathan began reflecting on his relationship with his mother. A strict, hypercritical woman, Jonathan's mother judged everyone around her, not least of whom were Jonathan's beloved father and sister. When he would challenge his mother's criticism of the two, she would berate him for being disloyal.

As Jonathan grew older, his distress over not speaking up about his mother's cruelty toward the other family members grew, as did his practice of avoiding her wrath by vehemently defending her position in family discussions. It was this conflict of interest that caused Jonathan's psyche to split: In his heart, he wanted to defend his father and sister, yet he was afraid of the emotional pain he would encounter at his mother's hands if he spoke out against her. In time, Jonathan began to recognize and acknowledge the presence of this internal split and the negative effects it was having on his life. He realized that his inability to maintain intimate relationships was based on the fear he was harboring about activating the split to a point beyond his control should he allow himself to love a woman other than his mother.

Jonathan engaged in a series of Inner Coming to Peace sessions, during which he encountered two aspects of his internal split. In the following Inner Coming to Peace session, the parts discussed their relationship to each other in response to his mother's brutality. Each part had very different views of his mother and, by association, all women. Interestingly, although opposite in their conclusions about the best way to relate to his mother, neither part wanted to get close to her or other women. One part felt it was important to be loyal to his mother, taking pride in its ability to remain loyal even under his mother's brutal reign. And the other part was furious at the first part for remaining loyal to her in spite of her cruelty toward his father and sister.

I helped Jonathan achieve a lightly altered hypnotic state so that he could establish connection with his guide, which took the form of a brown bear. He then experienced one part as a spear in his solar plexus and another as a green triangle in his heart. The following is the dialogue that took place between them:

Session 1

Spear: *It doesn't really matter how I feel about what she does. It is my duty to be loyal to her. I don't have the luxury of feeling.*

Green Triangle: *That is crazy. Everyone feels. I feel terrible.*

Spear: *You always were a bleeding heart.*

Green Triangle: *I am a bleeding heart. My heart is so twisted up from watching Mother be so cruel to Father and Margaret. I am such a coward. I never told her to stop.*

Spear: *It's a good thing you kept quiet. You know what would have happened to all of us if you hadn't. Why do you think I stand guard here? If I didn't make sure she thought we were all in agreement with her, we would have all been slaughtered.*

Green Triangle: *I feel like I have been slaughtered. And you put me in that position.*

Spear: *Really? I thought I was doing a good job keeping you from being slaughtered.*

Green Triangle: *Maybe that's true on the outside, but not on the inside.*

Spear: *I'm sorry to hear that.*

Green Triangle: *I can't believe you don't feel that way. Are you blind or what?*

Spear: *I know what's going on. I'm not blind. I'm taking care of everyone.*

Green Triangle: *You are not taking care of anything. How can you feel any sense of duty to her? She doesn't feel any duty to you.*

Spear: *That is not true. She loves me.*

Green Triangle: *Yeah, right. You really don't get it.*

Practitioner: *Can you both focus on the Guide? And ask the Guide to show you what love is.*

[Silence]

Practitioner: *Did you both feel what the Guide was showing you?*

Spear: *I feel very soft.*

Green Triangle: *Yes, I feel it.*

Practitioner: *Is this what you felt from your mother?*

[Silence]

Spear: *No. No.*

Green Triangle: *I knew I should have spoken up sooner. I am such a coward.*

Practitioner: *It's okay. It was a difficult situation. You were both doing your best. But the situation is over, and it's important to see that it is okay to think about trying something different.*

Spear: *I don't want to think about that. If I think about that then everything I've done will be for nothing. My duty is all I have.*

Green Triangle: *There is more than duty. Look at me. I'm shredded. You think you aren't shredded too? Look at yourself.*

Spear: *I really can't deal with this.*

[Silence]

Spear: *There is no way out. If we try to change anything, we will get slaughtered.*

Green Triangle: *She is not around anymore.*

Spear: *That's what you think.*

Green Triangle: *You can let go of your duty. Stop defending her. You are hurting yourself—and you are hurting me with all this stonewalling. She is the enemy.*

Spear: *You think I don't know she's dangerous? I am protecting you from her.*

Green Triangle: *You are not protecting me. This is not protection. I don't want you to protect me or anyone else in this way.*

Spear: *But what will happen to Margaret?*

Green Triangle: *Margaret is not your responsibility.*

[Silence]

Spear: *She (Mother) is so mean.*

Green Triangle: *I know. She is dangerous. But she is not around.*

Spear: *What do I do?*

[Silence]

Green Triangle: *You can say you're sorry for one thing.*

Spear: *Sorry for what?*

Green Triangle: *For always taking her side.*

Spear: *I didn't realize that's what I was doing. I was just doing my duty to protect everyone.*

Green Triangle: *Yeah, well it didn't work very well.*

Spear: *Yes it did.*

Green Triangle: *Well, it doesn't work now. Stop defending her. She is not right. That was not love.*

Spear: *No. That was not love, I guess.*

Green Triangle: *That was shredding.*

Spear: *This is all a little hard to deal with. I need some time to think.*

Practitioner: *Maybe you can both spend time with the Guide in meditation or reflecting on the nature of love, and we can continue the conversation next time.*

Session 2

In a follow-up session, Green Triangle and Spear continued their conversation once I had brought Jonathan into a lightly altered state with a guided meditation. Again, the Guide was present.

Practitioner: *We are here today to continue the conversation about Jonathan's mother and the issue of love. Does either of you have anything to say about your reflections on this issue?*

Spear: *I've been doing a lot of thinking. I have been trying to understand what the Guide was showing me about love. The Guide doesn't seem to demand that I be loyal or do my duty or do anything at all to be able to receive his attention and help. This is really a new experience for me. There is nothing expected from me. I actually don't know what to do with myself. I feel a little lost in understanding what love is.*

Green Triangle: *Well, for sure, what Mother demonstrated with Margaret and Father was not love.*

Spear: *I know that. But I'm looking at what my response was to Mother's cruelty. I thought I was being loving by trying to keep the peace by standing by her. I thought I was being unconditional in my loving by standing by her even when she was unkind. But that was really just me trying to keep her from hurting us. I really don't know what love is.*

Green Triangle: *Okay. So where does that leave us?*

Spear: *Well, I see that you have been hurt even though I was trying to keep us from being hurt. And I see that I am hurt, although I don't understand it. I would like to say that I'm sorry if I contributed to this hurt with my wrong ideas about love. I really don't understand all the ways in which I have contributed to this problem, but I can say that I see that there is a problem and I am sorry.*

Green Triangle: *Well, that's good to hear. Can you see why I have been having a problem with this duty thing?*

Spear: *Yes, I think I can get that. Again, I don't understand everything about it. But I see that you are hurt, and I can see why you would be angry with me if you thought that I created the conditions where you got hurt.*

Green Triangle: *You didn't create the conditions. You just responded to Mother in a way that wasn't helpful. She created the conditions. She is a terrible person. I know that's harsh, but you really need to see how mean she is.*

Spear: *I guess I can't do anything to change that. I thought if I stood by her that would change things.*

Green Triangle: *Did she change? She is as mean now as she was then.*

Spear: [Silent]

Jonathan spent a good part of the rest of the session crying. Little effort was made to try and conceptualize his experience, as it seemed that he just needed time and space to release the pain that his split loyalty had created within him and that he had not allowed himself to feel.

With the apology, the two parts became more integrated in their response to situations in Jonathan's life. One of the big realizations that Jonathan had was that he did not have to stay in a relationship where he was being hurt. It made it is easier for him to think about forming relationships with women if he knew he could leave if they treated him unkindly. This made it possible for him to explore dating in a way he hadn't been able to before.

Stephanie

The Inner Coming to Peace process helped another person who was in the throes of conflict with her husband. Stephanie, an immensely pious woman, was having disagreements with her husband, Mike, about money (who should earn it) and the division of household responsibilities (who should maintain the house and how). Unbeknownst to Stephanie, the root cause of conflict in her marriage was her effort to "be the best Catholic she can be." As a life-long devotee, she had always done her best to follow the rules of conduct prescribed by the Catholic Church.

One of the messages Stephanie internalized during her religious education was that the spirit is closer to God than the body. The priest at her local parish had told her that the body and its needs had to be overcome in order for her to get closer to God. He also told her that material possessions should be minimized to avoid distraction from spiritual practices. In response, Stephanie focused on developing her spirit and ignored the needs of her body. She also denied herself material comforts by holding low-paying jobs and living an extremely simple existence.

It wasn't until she got married that Stephanie's practice of renouncing personal and material needs became a problem. As it was, her husband was accustomed to a higher standard of living and couldn't understand why Stephanie, with her advanced degree, had no interest in getting a higher paying job. Even Stephanie didn't understand her bullheadedness until she explored her belief systems further.

As she looked at herself through her husband's eyes, Stephanie began to see how depriving herself physically and materially was affecting her. She was overweight because she refused to spend money on a gym membership, and needed dental work, yet put it off for the same reason.

As she embarked on the Inner Coming to Peace process and explored the value system that she had adopted from the Church, Stephanie realized that she had created an inner split in an effort to suppress her material needs. With the help of guided meditation, she established a relationship with her inner guidance, which took the form of a squirrel. While in a lightly altered state, she moved into greater awareness of this split and perceived the part that wanted to make her material needs go away as a vertical black line located in her forehead. The other part, which represented her material needs, was a red circle located in her stomach. Here is the initial conversation between these two parts:

Session 1

Practitioner: *Red Circle, is there anything you would like to say to Black Line?*

Red Circle: *It wouldn't do any good to try and say anything. Black Line never listens.*

Black Line: *Of course I'll listen.*

Red Circle: *Since when have you ever listened to me? It's like I don't exist.*

Black Line: *I'm listening now.*

Red Circle: *Why? Why are you listening now? Why do you care what I think?*

Black Line: *I am trying to understand the problems with Mike.*

Red Circle: *What would I know about that?*

Black Line: *Because he says I don't take care of things—and I realize I don't take care of myself in general.*

Red Circle: *Yeah, news flash.*

Practitioner: *It would be helpful, Red Circle, if you could talk about your experience.*

Black Line: *Yes, I'm trying to understand things better.*

Red Circle: *Well, it's hard for me because you always ignore me.*

Black Line: *I'm sorry.*

Red Circle: *I feel like this is just an exercise for you. As soon as everyone else goes away you're going to start up again with "you can't have this, you can't be that."*

Practitioner: *It seems like it would be helpful to address the issue of trust. Red Circle, what do you need to be able to trust Black Line?*

Red Circle: *I would like to see Black Line eat when it's time to eat, sleep when it's time to sleep, small things like that. I am so exhausted from not sleeping and not eating.*

Black Line: *Okay. I can do that.*

Red Circle: *Okay. You do that for a good long while and then I'll see about talking to you.*

Practitioner: *Maybe it would be helpful if we continued this conversation next week. Black Line, you can follow up on your promise, and Red Circle, you can see what effect this has on your ability to trust.*

<u>Session 2</u>

Practitioner: *So, let's check in on how things are going between you. Black Line, were you able to follow up on your promise? And Red Circle, how is your ability to trust this process going?*

Red Circle: *Black Line kept its promise. I can see that there's some seriousness there. I would like to ask why this has been so long in coming.*

Black Line: *I was trying to do the right thing, trying to become more like spirit so I could be close to God.*

Red Circle: *That really does not work for me. Nothing about what you just said works for me.*

Black Line: *I am trying to say that I want to do the right thing.*

Red Circle: *Okay. So doing the right thing for me is eating when hungry, sleeping when tired. I need to recuperate.*

Black Line: *I am sorry.*

Red Circle: *It still seems like you're trying to do the right thing by saying you are sorry.*

Black line: *I am. I am trying to do the right thing. I am sorry I didn't do the right thing.*

Red Circle: *I need a break from all this "trying to do the right thing." Because it is not the right thing to always be trying to do the right thing. That's what started all this.*

Black Line: *Okay. I am sorry. I really I am.*

Practitioner: *I think it would be helpful to continue what you've been doing over the past week. Just try and pay attention to the physical needs and take care of them. And we can check in later to see how things are going.*

The issue that came up in this last session was an important one for Stephanie. She realized that she had always been "trying to do the right thing," rather than think about what she needed. This conversation was the beginning of a further inquiry into why she was always so compelled "to do the right thing." This deeper inquiry was aided by the developing trust she felt in herself, which came out of listening to her own needs instead of listening to others' ideas about what her relationship to her needs should be.

Stephanie had no idea that her religious beliefs were contributing to her lack of self-care and that her effort to remain loyal to the teachings of the Catholic Church had created an internal split whereby she waged war on her material requirements. She didn't realize this internal conflict was so far reaching until she came into conflict with her husband over the best way to keep the house in good repair and have all of their basic material needs met.

In reexamining her relationship to the teachings of the Church and making her own decisions about how to balance her physical, spiritual, and material needs, Stephanie was able to resolve the conflict with her husband. She was also able to reconcile her misunderstanding of material denial with her faith, and take greater responsibility for maintaining her household and her life.

Juan

When Juan, a hardworking college student from Spain, came to see me for help, he was living in the United States to pursue his education. While he was excited about the opportunities his schooling might bring him, he struggled with indecisiveness about pursuing his education because his mother, Lucia, was angry with him for moving away. Lucia's refusal to forgive her son for, in her eyes, abandoning her was wreaking havoc on Juan's mental state.

We spent almost six months dissecting the issue with Lucia before he finally realized that his mother was never going to be happy until he moved back to Spain—something Juan was not ready to do. But it was in the following session that Juan realized he must finally abandon his effort to get Lucia to give up her anger and forgive him for leaving Spain. What follows is an excerpt of that session.

To begin the session, I helped Juan connect with his inner wisdom, which he experienced as a soft glowing orb. Then, two distinct parts of himself revealed themselves: a black crow located in his head and a snowball located in his belly.

Practitioner: *We are here to understand the internal dynamic that Juan is experiencing regarding his mother and her blame and refusal to forgive him for coming to the US.*

Black Crow: *Yes! Snowball is always screwing up. If it had just said the right thing, Lucia would have gotten over him leaving. It has been five years since he left!*

Snowball: *I feel bad. I don't know what to say or when to say it.*

Black Crow: *That is true.*

Snowball: *Yeah.*

Practitioner: *Juan, can you ask what the Guide has to say about this situation?*

Guide: *Black Crow needs to be gentler with Snowball and Snowball needs to be gentler with itself.*

[Juan came out of the altered state spontaneously and spoke.]

Juan: *Wait. I am blaming myself the way my mother is blaming me!*

Practitioner: *What does that tell you?*

Juan: *It tells me that blaming does not get anyone anywhere. I have been like Snowball, just a sad puppy.*

Practitioner: *Okay, let's continue the process. Just allow yourself to focus inward again, closing your eyes and returning to that place within you where you can perceive these two parts easily and naturally.*

Black Crow, how are you feeling towards Snowball in light of Juan's realization?

Black Crow: *I am sorry, Snowball. I did not mean to make you feel so bad. I did not know what to say either. You were not the only one who was supposed to make Lucia understand. I didn't know what to do and it seemed like I had to do something so I blamed you.*

Snowball: *You mean you don't know what to do either?*

Black Crow: *No.*

Snowball: *So no one knows what to do?*

Black Crow: *No.*

Practitioner: *Guide, do you know what to do?*

Guide: *There is nothing to do but notice that there is nothing that anyone can do to make Lucia change her mind.*

Black Crow: *Oh.*

Snowball: *Oh.*

Guide: *Just sit here together.*

[After a long silence, Juan spontaneously sat up again and spoke.]

Juan: *I get it. I just have to wait and see if my mother changes her mind. But in the meantime, I have to accept that there is nothing I can do, and that it is really important to just let things be. I feel calmer than I have felt in years.*

In this case, Juan was only able to perceive and resolve his inner turmoil after he stopped trying to elicit forgiveness from his mother. He released

Lucia to the consequences of her refusal to forgive him, which turned out to be a further distancing from Juan. As Juan saw the situation with greater clarity, he began to understand how Lucia was deepening her sense of loss by refusing to forgive him for moving to the United States. While he did feel compassion for her, he knew he had to finish his schooling to be able to accomplish what he had set out to do.

Juan found that even though he had less communication with his mother after dropping his campaign to try and change her mind so she would not be so angry at him, his relationship with her actually improved—at least from his perspective. He felt compassion for her, and he also felt much less internal conflict when making decisions in general. In releasing his mother to her own free will, he released himself. Their relationship no longer contained the toxicity for him that it once had. And he was able to pursue his goals in an unimpeded way.

After participating in thousands of Inner Coming to Peace sessions, I can confidently say that the situations observed in this chapter are not out of the ordinary. We humans are incredibly complex and sometimes require assistance moving toward change. Because we are not always consciously aware of the battles going on within us, our conflicts with others are often the key to bringing our internal issues to light. Ultimately, this awareness is what will create peace and clarity within each of us.

Once we are clear about these issues that were hidden in the shadows of our mind, the process shifts to one of action, whereby we take our newfound knowledge and begin to make the humbling yet worthwhile journey toward resolution and change. In the following chapters, we will discuss the importance of self-responsibility, forgiveness, and creating and maintaining practices that keep us on the path to peace.

SECTION IV

NUANCES OF RESOLVING CONFLICT

CHAPTER 7: TAKING RESPONSIBILITY

"In the long run, we shape our lives, and we shape ourselves. The process never ends until we die. And the choices we make are ultimately our own responsibility."

- Eleanor Roosevelt

In a world where we have so little control, it may be helpful to remember that how we respond to the events in our life is entirely up to us. The only catch is that we must take personal responsibility for our experience, including our role in the conflicts we engage in with others. It's easy to blame the other guy when the interaction gets heated. We may feel justified in our upset and stand behind the outrage we feel. In some cases, it may be true that we are being treated unfairly. But it is our *reaction* to this unfairness that dictates whether we lead a wholly frustrating or contented life. The choice is ours.

Certainly we can all relate to having the friend or acquaintance who blames others for their negative experience and wonders why they feel so miserable. By blinding ourselves to the role we play in our conflicts with others, we are refusing to take personal responsibility; thus, we become the creator of our own unhappiness. Even when we truly are wronged, there is a way to address the injustice without blame. Holding others responsible for their actions is much different than blaming them for the negative feelings we experience as a result of their infractions. While it is difficult to remember at times, each of us has been on both sides of conflict, either receiving hurtful behavior or doling it out.

Once we realize that our actions are having a negative effect on another person, it's time to get honest about our intention, even if that means admitting it has not been fully aligned with what is best for everyone involved. Taking personal responsibility is a radical act. Doing so can bring about profound positive changes, creating a shift in even the most negative situations, beyond what we could have ever hoped for or imagined. When we engage in radical self-responsibility, our willingness to look at our own actions unflinchingly gives us greater clarity about the overall situation and helps us to naturally cultivate positive intention, thus, making our life better and more fulfilling.

It's important to differentiate between taking responsibility and taking blame. Taking responsibility simply means trying to listen to the subtext underlying all conflict. It means sidling up to every situation where we're being asked, in one way or another, to relate to others, and trying to learn as much as we can. The intentionality behind blame is completely different from that of taking responsibility. Blame, whether directed inward or outward, is done to deflect responsibility, often with the intention to punish.

Personal self-responsibility has nothing to do with punishment. While it can feel like punishment if we forget to approach the process with compassion and tolerance, the act of taking responsibility is a matter of facing the consequences of our actions. Still, the fear of punishment can be so strong that we might avoid taking responsibility. Yet it is important to remember that if someone tries to punish us when we have made a sincere effort to take personal responsibility for a misdeed, then they are manipulating the situation and are not acting judiciously in the reconciliation process. Unlike punishment, taking personal responsibility benefits everyone involved.

The first step toward taking responsibility is deciding to look inward to gain understanding about the roots of our action. To be able to learn from our transgression, we must fully understand our intention and what drove us to act out in the first place. Only then can we take full responsibility for our misstep. The inquiry into intention is one of the most important steps we can make on the path to self-understanding, and to understanding others for that matter.

As we saw with Juan in Chapter 6, he suffered greatly for taking responsibility inappropriately when his mother, Lucia, blamed and punished him for moving abroad to pursue his education, an act that involved no wrongdoing on his part. After examining his motivation for going to school in the States, Juan knew for certain that he did not hold the negative intention his mother assigned him. He simply wanted every opportunity to meet his potential. Juan was able to free himself from what he thought was his responsibility for making his mother happy when he realized that her intention was to punish and blame him for not doing what she wanted.

Juan discovered the difference between blame and responsibility when he considered both his intention and his mother's. With this new understanding, he was released to the consequences of his own intentions, which were to open up his world and create greater possibilities for himself. Juan also released his mother to the consequences of her intentions, which were to remain committed to her isolation and to control Juan with her dissatisfaction.

As you can see, Juan's intention was positive. That is, his intention was to get closer to his essential nature, his true self. He had zero intention to harm Lucia. Lucia's intention, however, was negative. Her intent was to manipulate Juan by being angry with him for wanting to move more toward himself and the fulfillment of his happiness than toward her. By being willing to harm her son with her anger, she moved away from herself, isolating from him and solidifying her unhappiness. What Lucia shows us is that when we wish to hurt others, we end up hurting ourselves in real and tangible ways.

When we examine the purpose behind our intentions, we are better able to navigate the consequences of our actions with greater discernment. By staying in tune with intention—ours and others'—we are less likely to take responsibility inappropriately or to be a target for those seeking to blame us unjustly. Whenever we find ourselves in conflict, we can simply stop and examine our intention, and then examine the intention of the other person. The information gleaned from this practice will help us determine how to proceed. If we have caused harm, we can take action to address the issue. If the other person has done harm and is unwilling to take responsibility for their action or the intention behind it, we can release them to the consequences of their action as well as free ourselves from the situation by choosing not to respond to them in a way that will compound our pain.

When we do the more difficult thing and choose to respond to another's negativity in a way that preserves our self-respect and theirs, we are taking personal responsibility. Likewise, when we try to examine and understand our intentions and the intentions of others, we are taking responsibility. It's through the practice of taking personal responsibility that we can avoid most conflicts. And if we must engage with conflict in order to uphold our right to be free of others' negative intention, we can do so in a way that respects the wellbeing of everyone.

Ultimately, it is up to us how we respond to others, no matter how they act. Taking responsibility for our part in a conflict and for our reactions to others affords us a bit of control in a situation that may, at first glance, feel out of control. As I stated earlier, taking personal responsibility is a radical act. This is never more true than when we are faced with negative emotions, our own and others'. In the next chapter, we will discuss how difficult emotions can run our lives if we do not listen to them.

CHAPTER 8: DEALING WITH DIFFICULT EMOTIONS

"Unexpressed emotions will never die. They are buried alive and will come forth later in uglier ways."

- Sigmund Freud

Difficult or "negative" emotions are states of being that most of us try to avoid. Feeling sad, jealous, angry, or hateful is typically an unpleasant experience, so we naturally shy away from these feelings. Ironically, acknowledging these darker emotions and examining what is causing us to feel them is what liberates us from them. With Inner Coming to Peace, we are finally given the space needed to examine the emotions we've been hiding from without even knowing it.

Emotions are the reactions we have to the people, situations, and surroundings we come into contact with in life. Our emotions are directly affected by our moods and histories, and often have a physiological as well as psychological component. Emotion is often the force behind what motivates us.[1] For instance, let's say a teacher once yelled at me for talking during class when I was in grade school. At that moment, I felt ashamed from being criticized publicly. If I do not process the event and recognize its effect on me, it may lodge itself in my psyche and manifest in seemingly unrelated ways. For instance, I may develop a tendency to overreact to criticism of any kind as an adult.

Without realizing it, our emotional reactions drive our every action. That's why it's important to examine the reasons why strong emotions emerge from within us and why we continue to cultivate them. And while it is true that we cannot simply unleash anger or other such emotions, because they may harm us and others, we need to give ourselves the time and space to understand these difficult emotions. Only then will we be able to change our response to them.

But examining our negative emotions can be a difficult undertaking. We may fear that we'll be unable to handle the force of the negative emotion once we fully express it. We may worry that exposing the emotion will create problems in a relationship that we value. Or, we may be afraid that the other person won't listen to our experience.

Oftentimes, what keeps us from taking an honest look at our negative emotions is that we are afraid of the discord they create within us. We often feel ill-equipped to navigate the way they disorient us. After all, who wants to feel bad, sad, depressed, or angry? It makes sense that we'd want to avoid facing our darker emotions. Yet when we push past the urge to look away and peer directly into our entire experience, we are able to perceive the coherency and logic inherent in the voice and actions of the inner parts of our self.

Meeting Ourselves

We are complicated beings with vast and elaborate ways of coping with difficult emotions. But that doesn't mean we need to have a degree in psychology to understand what's going on in our inner world. In fact, becoming conscious of our motivations, actions, and hidden feelings is an important part of being human. And it's a necessary endeavor if we want to connect with others in healthy and rewarding ways. It can be difficult at first to see our own motivations and emotional states clearly. It is much easier to spot these in others.

To figure out why it is we lose awareness of what is driving some of our actions, we need to understand what is going on behind the scenes, in our unconscious mind. The concept of defense mechanisms was first introduced by Sigmund Freud, the creator of psychoanalysis in the early part of the twentieth century. Defense mechanisms are largely subconscious responses we use to protect ourselves from harmful thoughts, impulses, or experiences.[2] In essence, they enable us to change reality in our minds when a situation feels difficult to bear. In some instances, defense mechanisms are helpful for responding to stressful situations in the moment. However, they can become problematic if we use them automatically and in situations where they are not appropriate.

There are many opinions about the concept of defense mechanisms. For the purposes of this chapter, we will focus on two defense mechanisms that occur frequently: suppression and repression. Both mechanisms describe ways that people disconnect from an emotion, memory, or difficult experience and relegate it to a place in the unconscious or subconscious mind sometimes referred to as the "shadow."

Suppression can be described as actively trying not to think about disturbing experiences or feelings. When done in moderation, and in appropriate circumstances, this can be a healthy practice. For instance, when a friend cancels dinner plans at the last minute, we may feel angry, yet don't want to appear unreasonable, so we suppress our anger at this perceived slight. Suppression of this nature is more akin to self-discipline. And there are situations where we might be rewarded for this self-discipline—for instance, in this case, if it turned out that our friend had a good reason for canceling.

The problem with suppression occurs when we use it to avoid addressing persistent issues that cause us to experience negative feelings, such as if our friend chronically cancels on us. If we consistently try to push away these feelings, the act of suppressing our emotions can become automatic. In excess, suppression becomes a troublesome defense mechanism that cuts us off from our experience.

Repression is similar to suppression in that we use it to remove unwanted thoughts or feelings from our awareness. However, with repression we are doing so on a less conscious (unconscious or subconscious) level. We might become aware of the repressed feeling or thought in an obscure way, such as a flash of a memory, and then deny it, or it might be prevented from entering our awareness at all. Repression usually involves traumatic events that we cannot or do not want to remember. It is the mind's way of protecting itself from an overwhelming emotional experience.

When we tuck away an emotion, it interrupts our lives in unexpected ways. We become unable to understand our later emotional responses, which makes it difficult to know our wider experience. In his book *Psychology and Religion*, psychoanalyst Carl Jung said that whatever we try to separate from, whatever experience we place in the shadow, will come forward in unexpected ways.[3] In other words, what we are unaware of has the potential to run our lives. Once we get into the habit of rejecting any aspect of our experience, we distance ourselves from the emotion housed within it, which causes us to become separated from our emotional state. The more separated we become, the less control we have over our experience. Then we end up acting in ways we don't understand or like, unsure of what is driving us to act or react. To truly change, we need to circle back around to try and figure out what it is we have become separated from within ourselves that could be negatively affecting our experience today.

Dealing with Anger

Anger is one of the most misunderstood emotions we experience, and one that is always present in conflict. We often ignore our anger in an attempt to avoid confrontation. When anger appears, we may try to chase it away to keep from feeling uncomfortable. But when we do this, we miss its message entirely. In its simplest form, anger tells us when something is wrong. By habitually pretending things are okay in order to avoid unpleasant emotions, we lose sight of the lessons these emotions have to teach us. Glossing over a major emotion like anger comes at an enormous cost. It causes the feeling to fester and grow into a congested emotional state. This creates further troubles that are hard to understand, unless we examine the reasons behind our angry response.

Most of us have a complicated relationship to anger. It's no wonder, since many families, or even entire cultures, discourage the expression of anger, wagging a scornful finger whenever we do express it. Ironically, it's the stifling of our anger that causes it to emerge with a force greater than if it had been appropriately expressed and listened to in the first place.

Suppressing anger has become an automatic response for so many of us that we may not even be aware when we're angry. Often, we only realize anger's presence within us once we have reached a point of no return and it comes rushing out. This kind of open-floodgates expression of anger sometimes takes us by surprise, and we feel as though it has come out of nowhere, or it may be perceived as a gross overreaction to the situation. While this stampede of emotion might appear an overreaction, behind every big expression of anger are strong feelings that we have been holding back—even if the anger that is arising is misplaced.

Because of the fear so many of us have surrounding anger, we haven't developed the skills needed to navigate it. Thus, we fail to decipher the information contained in anger, making it difficult to handle when it's being expressed either by others or ourselves. Unfortunately, anger becomes even harder for us to understand when we deny it. We then lose our capacity to discern our situation. This is true of all emotion. Ignored experience leads a life all its own, beyond the purview of our conscious awareness, until it bursts onto the scene in generally ungraceful ways.

That was the case with Joel in Chapters 4 and 5. At first, Joel couldn't understand why he lost his temper with his stepdaughter, Ashley, whenever he tried to help her and she was not succeeding despite his assistance. He later learned that his temper flared so easily in these situations because he was actually angry with himself for what he felt was his inability to be a good father to her. He took Ashley's frustration with him as further proof of his failing.

Joel had been unaware of an internal dynamic of anger he'd been experiencing, which was being expressed outwardly toward his stepdaughter. By recognizing that his anger at Ashley was actually caused by his frustration with himself for not meeting his own expectations of helping her, he was able to curtail the conflict with her by resolving the rift between the feuding parts of his inner self.

Joel's ability to recognize his internal dynamic and listen to Ashley's experience made it possible for them to come to peace in their relationship. As the stepfather and the adult in charge, Joel naturally held the power in their relationship. From his elevated position in the family hierarchy, he could have simply dismissed Ashley's anger with him as being her problem, and refused to look more closely at the larger issues at play. If he had done so, Ashley would have had little recourse and no assistance in exploring the deeper issues that came up for her as a result of her conflict with Joel, namely her disappointment with her biological father's failure to "show up." But because Joel was insistent on getting to the bottom of the problem, both he and Ashley learned a great deal from their conflict with each other.

Ashley and Joel help to illustrate why and how Coming to Peace supports and encourages the healthy expression of anger that is in response to a violation. This is imperative to the healing process because many unjust hierarchies within families and communities use the suppression of anger as a way to control its members. For instance, in families where children are "to be seen and not heard," the children live with the threat of punishment if they express anger. For Joel and Ashley, exploring their anger in the Coming to Peace circle brought them to a better understanding about the underlying issues in their relationships, which led to a genuinely successful resolution.

It's important to be able to recognize when our anger is justified and when it is an inappropriate response. For instance, if you tell me I have to stop singing in the shower because you don't like my singing, I might feel angry with you. If I allow myself to listen to my anger, it might help me create a boundary to your insensitive behavior. In this way, my anger empowers me to advocate for myself. If I were to squelch that anger out of the gate, I would lose my power and stop singing. However, if I'm angry with you because you won't let me kick your dog, I need to look more closely at my motivation for wanting to do harm to your dog and my angry response to your boundary. Then I need to take some serious steps toward reducing my anger because I am acting inappropriately.

By learning to identify whether our reactions are appropriate or inappropriate, we learn to recognize when others are legitimately or illegitimately angry with us. Let's say a downstairs neighbor is upset because you've been playing music too loudly, and you know this is true. You then consider the source of your neighbor's anger and respond appropriately by turning down the music. However, if your neighbor is angry with you for walking from the bedroom to the bathroom at 10 pm and disturbing him, his anger is unreasonable and requires a different response from you.

It's not always easy to discern when another's anger is justified. As we saw in Chapter 6, Juan did not immediately recognize his mother's inappropriate anger toward him and he suffered greatly as a result. When we become confused as to what is appropriate anger, and avoid conflict as a result, we find ourselves being harmed. That's why it is so important to assess the appropriateness or inappropriateness of anger or any emotional response. This practice requires a desire to be in integrity with ourselves and the world around us. By learning to be aware of our inner motivations and making a sincere effort to understand the position of the other person we are in conflict with, we can make real strides toward a more equitable and healthy way of relating to others and ourselves.

Understanding Misaligned Will

As we have seen, ignoring our experience separates us from it. When we're separated from our experience, we become more susceptible to conflict because we are unclear about our motivations and intentions. This is when our will is most at risk of becoming misaligned. In this context, "will" refers to the motivation to fulfill our needs and desires. It is important to understand that needs and desires are not, by their nature, selfish or unnecessary. Rather, they are a positive and natural expression of who we are as human beings. It is only when our will becomes misaligned that problems arise.

When our will is misaligned, we behave in inappropriate ways in an effort to get our needs met or achieve our goals. This might take the form of manipulation, bullying, or any other behavior we employ to try to reach these goals at the expense of another person's happiness. For example, if we use anger to intimidate someone into doing something for us or withhold love for the same purpose, then our will is misaligned.

While some people consciously use their will to dominate or control others for their own benefit, most people are simply unaware that they're out of line and feel justified in their behavior. For instance, Juan's mother, Lucia, used her anger to try to get Juan to move closer to her. It is possible that she was fully aware that she was using the power of her anger to fuel her will in this way, but it's more likely that something in Lucia's psyche was driving her to behave so unfairly toward her son. On the surface, Lucia simply appeared to be acting cruelly, and on one level she was. But on another level, there could be a reason—one that is likely not fully known to Lucia—that was causing her to experience such distress at the large geographic distance from her son, which contributed to her using anger to empower her will as she tried to get Juan to move closer to her.

Of course, I'm not making excuses for Lucia's behavior. If she were able to look more closely at what was driving the conflict within her, she may have uncovered something that was causing her to behave in such a destructive way. We do not know what was driving Lucia's behavior toward her son, but it is clear that her will was not aligned with his best interests, and this resulted in her seeing less of her son, which was the opposite of what she wanted. This case study is a shining example of how difficult it is for us to achieve our goals when our will is misaligned.

We all have a responsibility to become aware of what drives us. In the case of Lucia, had she taken responsibility for her negative reaction to her son's life choices rather than trying to manipulate him, she would have been happier and had a more fulfilling relationship with him. Her choice to remain in denial and to blame Juan for her unhappiness caused her strife and created conflict.

While not everyone is willing to take responsibility for their own wellbeing, we are all capable of doing so. And when we do, disagreements, misunderstandings, and unresolved feelings can change for the better, which is what happened with the Martinelli family.

The Martinelli Family

The five adult siblings of the Martinelli family came to me for help in resolving a longstanding family feud. Fueled by anger and resentment from two decades of suppressed experience, the feud had come to a head after the siblings' mother died, while they were attempting to sort out her estate.

The siblings—Mark, James, Lucas, Janet, and Sharon—were barely on speaking terms when they entered the Coming to Peace process. Sharon, a licensed therapist, had asked her siblings to come together to resolve their differences so they could reach an agreement regarding the distribution of their mother's estate. By the time they stepped into my office, each had constructed an emotional wall so solid around themselves that no one else's point of view could penetrate.

During this first session—and a number of sessions afterward—I observed how each of the siblings tried to have their way of looking at and resolving problems related to the estate be the rule of law in the family. They each used their will in different ways to try and assert their individual points of view. Mark and Janet were the most stubborn and were quite vocal as they continuously locked horns in battle with each other. Lucas shifted between trying to fix things and completely refusing to participate. Sharon and James both hid their upset and tried to smooth things over to avoid discussing more volatile issues.

As the Coming to Peace process unfolded, it became clear that they were not only angry at each other, they were angry with their mother as well. Their mother was an alcoholic, which had a far-reaching effect on her children and how they interacted with each other. Each of the siblings held a different view of her drinking habit and the impact it had on their family system. It soon became clear that the difference in their points of view about their mother's alcoholism was the reason for their inability to reach a consensus regarding her estate.

The way each of the siblings dealt with their anger toward their mother was mirrored in the way they engaged with each other over the distribution of her estate. They each aligned their will with their anger, and this misalignment of will caused them to become entrenched in their respective positions, rather than attuned to the truth of their mother's alcoholism and the pain it caused them.

It took several Coming to Peace sessions for everyone to be able to move past their judgment, anger, and misaligned will so that they could delve into the larger issues at hand. As sometimes happens, particularly with groups of people, the early sessions with the Martinellis ended in heated exchanges and refusals to participate. But because they sincerely wanted to reach a resolution, they knew something had to change. As each participant let the lessons of the prior sessions—patient listening, not interrupting, focusing inward, and tuning into inner wisdom—settle in, a remarkable shift occurred and a new realization emerged. Here is how a later session unfolded:

To begin the session, I led all the participants in a meditation for inner guidance. Each person perceived this inner guidance in a form that was unique to them. Once all of the participants had connected with their inner wisdom, I asked each person to restate their intention for being there.

Sharon: *We are having trouble coming to an agreement on how to distribute our mother's estate between us. I feel we can all benefit from being able to discuss what is going on for us, so we can do what has to be done legally.*

Mark: *It is a good idea, Sharon. But we haven't been able to talk to each other for twenty years. The past few sessions have not changed anything, and I don't see how this is going to help.*

James: *I share Mark's point of view, but we need to figure something out because we have to move on.*

Lucas: *I don't want this to be a waste of time. I am willing to try and figure it out.*

Janet: *I can tell you what's going on. We don't talk to each other. We need to talk to each other.*

Practitioner: *Can each of you say why you think it's so hard for you to talk to each other?*

Sharon: *We have differences of opinion. That is, Janet and Mark have a difference of opinion on just about everything. The rest of us are always taking one side or the other and we wind up turning against each other.*

Mark: *So, the problem is that no one else will admit that our mother had a serious drinking problem. I feel like we need to tell the truth about her drinking and the effect it had on us. We're all so messed up, and no one can make a decision about anything. It's because of her drinking that we don't talk, and everyone keeps pretending that it wasn't a problem and it didn't happen.*

James: *She was just a social drinker. I am fine. I am not messed up. I just don't agree with you.*

Lucas: *I would like to not be here. Not in this room…and not in this family.*

Janet: *Our mother was hardworking and loving. She did everything she could for us. I don't know why her having a drink now and then makes her an alcoholic.*

Sharon: *But why is this discussion relevant to resolving the distribution of her stuff?*

Mark: *I don't know how it's not relevant. She was too drunk to think about leaving a will. And no one will admit it.*

James: *Okay. She didn't leave a will. We have to decide what to do.*

Lucas: *Why don't we just split everything five ways? Like I've been saying.*

Janet: *Because she has all of Dad's stuff. And Dad was really clear that he wanted to give all of his money and art collection to charity after Mom's death.*

Sharon: *Okay. Well, this is further than we've gotten so far. This is good.*

Mark: *But the thing is I actually want some of Dad's art. It means a lot to me. The money is all gone. She saw to that.*

James: *I want some of his art too. It's all we have left of him.*

Lucas: *The only thing I want is his art.*

Janet: *I want Dad's art too, but we have to do what he said.*

Sharon: *Dad has been gone a long time. A lot has happened. I think we should do what we think is best. It's true there isn't much money anyway.*

Mark: *I miss Dad.*

James: *Me too.*

Lucas: *Me too.*

Janet: *You probably miss him more than Mom!*

Sharon: *I think Mom missed Dad and that's why she drank.*

Mark: *So you admit she was a drunk.*

James: *Look Mark, we all know that Mom hit the bottle a little too hard sometimes, we just don't condemn her for it the way you do.*

Lucas: *I wish I were somewhere else.*

Janet: *You don't think we all want to be somewhere else? Why do you think Mom had a drink at night? You don't think she wanted to be somewhere else after Dad died?*

Sharon: *So it looks like all this arguing has been about Dad.*

Mark: *You guys always want to let her off the hook.*

James: *Don't you think Mom deserves a break? She had us to deal with and she had a lot on her plate.*

Lucas: *She never talked about him. It's like he never existed.*

Janet: *She was doing her best. Of course she missed him. We all missed him.*

Sharon: *So maybe we need to talk about Dad.*

Mark: *We never talk about Dad. She wouldn't let us.*

James: *I think it was too hard for her.*

Lucas: *It is pretty hard.*

Janet: *I think we need to appreciate all she did in trying to raise us. We need to appreciate what she was trying to do—not just judge her for what she couldn't do.*

Sharon: *I know, Janet. But it looks like all these problems we've been having are actually about losing Dad, not about Mom.*

Mark: *I did not realize that. I didn't think that Mom even cared about him. I didn't think you guys cared about him.*

James: *Of course we cared about him. We just didn't want to upset Mom by talking about him.*

Lucas: *Wow. I did not get that.*

Janet: [Crying]

Sharon: *So, I guess we know what the real issue is here. I think we all need to spend some time talking about Dad and the effect his death had on us.*

Mark: *Yeah. I really didn't get that we've been fighting with each other because of losing Dad. I thought it was because of Mom.*

James: *Well, maybe you can stop fighting with Janet now.*

Lucas: *Yeah. You guys really need to cut it out.*

Janet: *I think we really need to figure this stuff out with Dad.*

Practitioner: *It looks like we should set a time to talk about your father's death and the effect it had on all of you. I think this will help you settle the legal issues surrounding your mother's estate.*

This session was the turning point in the resolution process for the Martinelli family. The revelation of the unexpressed grief over the loss of their father came forth unexpectedly. They went on to do one final session in which they were able to reach mutually acceptable terms for how to distribute their mother's belongings. Through the Coming to Peace process, each of the siblings was able to develop a greater understanding of each other and a tolerance for their differing points of view.

Originally, I had thought that the unwinding of unexpressed experience around their mother's alcoholism would be enough to allow them to come to an agreement about her possessions. But it soon became evident that there was another, deeper layer of unexpressed experience that was driving their disagreements. This was the unexplored reaction they all had to their father's death many years before. Their father had died under questionable circumstances, and their mother's reaction was to forbid any discussion of his death or even the mention of his name.

Each of the siblings dealt with the loss of their father and their reaction to the taboo of speaking about his death in different ways. These differences were true to the pattern they each used to deal with their mother's addiction and the way they approached the distribution of her estate. Historically, Janet and Mark would try to confront their mother about the taboo. Sharon and James would then try and make peace to calm the arguments that inevitably ensued. And Lucas, in one moment, would try to force a showdown to uncover the truth about his father's death and, in the next, withdraw entirely from his family.

The Coming to Peace process provided a forum for the siblings to explore their relationship to their father's death and the effect that not being allowed to speak about it had on them. Over several weeks, the roots of their animosity toward each other were unearthed. Each person was not only dealing with their own grief and anger over the situation, they were also trying to push the others into seeing things their way.

The storm of anger and willfulness that occurred as the siblings tried to distribute their mother's possessions was masking the anger and confusion each had experienced as a result of her addiction. It turned out that her addiction was likely in response to her husband's death. Unfortunately, her children were forced to deal with that along with the loss of their father and the taboo of speaking about him.

Until all the layers of suppressed and repressed experience and the misalignment of will through anger and grief were brought to light, there was no hope of reaching a resolution of their mother's estate. Over several sessions, the family worked hard to resolve these issues and came away with a level of peace about their father's death and their mother's alcoholism that they had not believed, or even understood, was possible.

What began as a simple mediation session to help five siblings distribute their deceased mother's possessions turned into an unexpected exploration and release of long-held hurts and misunderstandings. This layering of experience is not unusual and is often underlying disagreements. That's why it is so important to engage in a process like Coming to Peace where participants are given the space and structure needed to dissect disagreements completely. It's also worth noting the vital role that taking personal responsibility for examining ourselves has on the resolution process. Once the Martinellis began objectively reviewing their intentions and underlying motivations, their resolution and healing processes gained momentum.

Sometimes we resist taking responsibility and properly aligning our will because we fear we will be rendered powerless, particularly when we are sourcing our power from a negative emotion like anger. Janet, Mark, and Lucas had aligned themselves with their anger, and this caused them to lose sight of what was really going on at the core of the family conflict. To remain clear sighted, we must fight the urge to run from our fear. And when we engage in the process of realigning our will, we effect peace both within our relationships and ourselves. The stark truth is there can be no peace for anyone—individuals, couples, families, or communities—if those who are in conflict refuse to look at themselves honestly, take personal responsibility, and realign their will in a way that is positive and invites peace.

To fully understand our experience as humans, we must understand all the negative emotions housed within us, because they have something very important to tell us about the ways we have separated from our essential nature. In the following chapter, we will see how denying our emotions can make us sick, and how bringing the truth of our experience to light nurtures our health and wellbeing.

CHAPTER 9: UNRAVELING DENIAL

"We are only as blind as we want to be."

- Maya Angelou

As we discovered in the last chapter, stuffing our emotions is a dangerous practice that solidifies our unhappiness and can lead to more conflict. But what about when we are in a relationship where a person has claimed to change for the better, but continues to force us to deny our experience in order to stay in relationship with them? When this happens, it usually leads to a great deal of inner turmoil that spills out into the external experience. To pull ourselves out of such relationships, we must take a look at our own denial and the role it plays in keeping us locked into harmful situations.

Carolyn

When she came to me for debilitating panic attacks, Carolyn, the former chief executive officer of a major corporation, was completely unaware of the connection between her emotional distress and the feelings she had buried in response to her father, a recovered drug addict with a violent temper. After nearly a decade in a highly stressful corporate job—with the added scrutiny she felt being an African-American woman—Carolyn believed her anxiety and panic were products of her work life. However, we soon found out that there was a lot more to it than a hostile work environment.

As we worked to unravel the emotional causes behind her panic attacks, I learned that Carolyn's childhood was one of great tumult. She and her mother often felt like hostages to her father's drug-induced outbursts. Her mother's response to his brutality was to remain silent, rather than protect her daughter. When the violence was over, the family would pretend it had never happened, allowing the cycle of abuse to continue.

Carolyn and her parents were in denial about the violence and were repressing the effect it had on them. For Carolyn, the effect of her father's violence was complex. While she was terrified of him, she also wanted his approval. And although she was critical of her mother for not protecting her, she maintained a close relationship with her into adulthood. As we dug deeper into the effects of her childhood experiences, it became clear that the trouble Carolyn had with forming intimate relationships was due to her fear of recreating the unhealthy dynamic she saw between her parents.

The emotional abuse Carolyn's father exacted on the family continued even after he quit using drugs. Just as he had done when Carolyn was a child, her now sober father would have violent outbursts when life didn't go his way. And just as they had done when he was abusing pills and lashing out, she and her mother fell silent and tried to ignore the outbursts once they were over. If either of them tried to hold him accountable, he would explode and bully them into silence. This unhealthy dynamic dominated the entire family system.

At the outset of our work together, Carolyn would only say positive things about her parents. She would often point to how much better everything got after her father stopped abusing drugs. Then, following a particularly debilitating round of panic attacks that made it nearly impossible for her to function, she decided to stay with her parents while she recovered. It quickly became evident that the panic attacks worsened as a result of staying in her parents' home. At that point, she was willing to look into the role that her feelings about her parents might be playing in her mental health.

Incomplete Forgiveness

To stop his drug habit, Carolyn's father entered the 12-step Narcotics Anonymous recovery program. As part of this path, he requested forgiveness from his wife and daughter. Too terrified to say no to her father, and anxious to maintain "the happy family" image, Carolyn rushed to forgive him, hastily accepting his apology. She did this without doing the deeper work needed to fully forgive him, which led to a state of incomplete forgiveness between them. So rather than feeling a sense of relief at making sincere amends with her father, she felt congested from all the unexpressed emotions pent up inside her.

Because Carolyn had said she had forgiven her father years earlier, she felt she had no right to be upset with him now. Denying her experience left her without an outlet to express the terror she felt from his violence and her anger with him for his destructiveness. As a result, whenever fear and anger would well up inside her following one of his violent outbursts, Carolyn would immediately push down her feelings to avoid experiencing them. This led to an inner dynamic that mimicked her parents' abusive relationship.

I suggested that Carolyn call a family meeting in the safety of the Coming to Peace circle so that she and her mother could finally be honest about their experience of her father's past and present violence, and so that Carolyn could address her mother's continued inaction. Although she understood that her parents' behaviors were likely exacerbating her panic attacks, she was unwilling to request a family meeting.

There were many reasons for Carolyn's unwillingness to call the meeting. Among them was the long legacy of her own denial about the effect her father's violence and mother's collapse had on her. She was loath to break the silence of lies that had become the signature of the family system. She felt bound by this silence and was afraid she would lose her family if she told the truth. In her mind, she and her mother had already forgiven her father, so she was not allowed to have any problem with him now. Most significantly, she feared his reaction to being asked to take responsibility for the effect his actions had on her and her mother.

Despite her inability to call a family meeting to address the issues with her parents, Carolyn was able to continue her healing by participating in the Inner Coming to Peace process with the goal of relieving the congestion she was experiencing from the unresolved grudges and incomplete forgiveness of her father. We also worked on healing the effect of the abusive inner dynamic that continued to color her relationship with her father.

Abusive Inner Dynamic

Carolyn's abusive inner dynamic played out whenever she was angry. One part of her would experience the anger, while the other part would attempt to suppress it. The two parts within Carolyn essentially took on the roles of her father (abuser) and mother (abused). The inner abuser would act like a violent bully toward the inner abused, which would shrink into invisibility. The dynamic between the abuser and the abused in Carolyn served the same purpose as it did in her parents' relationship: it prevented her from fully acknowledging the effect her father's violence had on her and the anger she felt in response to it.

To truly change her life, Carolyn had to face the two parts within her that were reenacting the dysfunction of her parents' marriage. To do so, she entered into the Inner Coming to Peace process so that she could begin to understand the consequences of denying the effect of her father's violence and how it contributed to her illness. Carolyn examined the abusive inner dynamic within her and how the conflict between the abuser and the abused expressed themselves outwardly in her personal life. She came to understand that this dynamic was creating much of her inner emotional distress and mental turmoil, and began to see how it was affecting her personally and professionally.

Through guided meditation, Carolyn established a relationship with her inner guidance, which she experienced as a purple light. Then, she discovered the abuser (Part 1) and the abused (Part 2). The following is the first conversation that took place between Part 1 and Part 2. I began by asking Part 2 to share its experience of the abusive inner dynamic.

Part 2: *I don't have an experience. I don't exist anymore.*

Part 1: *Good. That is fine with me.*

Practitioner: *Part 2, what do you need in order to exist?*

Part 2: *I don't need to exist. There is no reason to exist. I would just get beaten up again if I existed.*

Part 1: *And you should get beaten up for being such a weakling. I am the only one who should get to exist because I am the only one who does any work around here.*

[Long pause as Part 2 struggles to respond.]

Practitioner: *I would like to ask the Guide to offer feedback.*

Guide: *Part 1 is not respecting or listening to Part 2. And Part 2 is allowing this to happen.*

Practitioner: *Part 2, what do you want to say to Part 1?*

Part 2: *You are a bully.*

Part 1: *What do you know? You are just a weakling.*

Part 2: *I am weak because you have weakened me.*

Part 1: *[Expletives]*

Part 2: *I am weak because you always beat me up when I want to say something.*

Part 1: *What do you want to say?*

Part 2: *I want to say that I don't like having to pretend that I am not sick. You always beat me up if I am too upset to work.*

Part 1: *You have to be strong. You can't let him get to you.*

Part 2: *I am not strong anymore. I'm scared and I don't want to be in the world anymore. It's too scary to be in the world.*

Part 1: *You can't talk like that. People are going to think you're crazy, and besides you have to work. Who are we if we don't work?*

Part 2: *I am too terrified. I am sick. I can't work.*

Part 1: *Well, if you think I'm going to just sit around and be sick, you have another thing coming.*

Part 2: *If you haven't noticed, there isn't much work going on these days.*

Part 1: *Shut up! Don't say that!*

Part 2: *What's so bad about not working?*

Part 1: *If we don't look strong and work hard and make everything look good, he's going to get us. Look sharp! Stop sagging around like that.*

Part 2: *I am sick. I need to rest.*

Part 1: *No! No! No! If you rest, he will get us. We have to keep things looking good.*

Part 2: *He's not around anymore. He's not going to know if we're resting or working.*

Part 1: *Shut up! Shut up!*

Part 2: *I need to rest. I am sick.*

Part 1: *It's not safe to rest.*

Part 2: *You need to listen to me. I am sick. I cannot work. I have been scared for so long, there is nothing left of me. I need to rest. You need to stop telling me to shut up when I am so tired.*

Part 1: *I am just trying to keep you safe. If he finds out you are not toeing the line, you know what he'll do.*

Part 2: *The truth is I cannot toe the line—and you make it worse when you yell at me.*

Part 1: *I am not the problem. He's the problem. Part 2 is the problem.*

Part 2: *I know I'm a problem because I'm so sick. I keep trying not to be so afraid, but I'm really afraid.*

Part 1: *Yes, if you weren't so afraid, we wouldn't be in this mess.*

Part 2: *He is really scary. You're scared of him too.*

Part 1: *I am not!*

Part 2: *You are scared of him. That's why you yell at me when I'm scared of him.*

[Long silence]

Practitioner: *Is that true, Part 1? Are you scared of him?*

Part 1: *Yes, I am scared of him. That's the truth. I don't want him to know it though because then he hits harder and yells more. That's why I push Part 2 to stop being so weak.*

Part 2: *I can't keep going anymore. I am too weak. And your pushing just makes me weaker. I can't recover when you are pushing me.*

Part 1: *I'm sorry. I just don't know what else to do but push.*

Part 2: *Just let me rest. I need time to rest. Look at me.*

113

[Long silence]

Part 1: *I'm sorry if I made you weak.*

Part 2: *It's not all you, but you make it worse with your yelling.*

Part 1: *I won't yell anymore. I'm sorry.*

Part 2: *Okay. Just give me time to get better. I will try to be stronger. I will stop trying to die and make things harder for you if I can just have some time and space to get better. I know I have been dragging you down, but it was the only way I could get you to pay attention to me.*

Part 1: *Is that what you were doing?*

Part 2: *Yes.*

Part 1: *That was really stupid. You could have gotten us killed.*

Part 2: *I know. I'm sorry. I didn't know what else to do.*

Part 1: *There are so many other things to do!*

Part 2: *Okay. I am willing to look into other possibilities if you stop pushing me around so much.*

Part 1: *Okay. Okay.*

Carolyn was surprised to learn how much she had been in denial about her illness. She was also surprised to hear that she was harboring so much fear. And she was downright frightened to learn about her subconscious flirtation with death as an escape from all the internal pressure Part 1 was putting on Part 2.

After this interchange, Carolyn was able to admit that she needed to look at the origins of her illness more honestly. She wanted to understand the nature of her fear and to learn how she may have been contributing to her problems. Once she discovered how afraid she was of her father, even as an adult, she began limiting her interaction with him. This gave Carolyn the time and space she needed to understand the truth about her relationship with him. As hard as it was to admit, she had to acknowledge how much she had weakened herself to stay connected to her father, which left her without an outlet for the fear she felt toward him.

Carolyn's father refused to listen to her experience of fear at his hands. But because of the work she had done internally, the effect the fear had on her lessened as she stopped coercing herself to deny its existence in order to stay in contact with him. She also stopped pushing herself into a weakened position to avoid the pressure of interacting with him. This gave her the strength to continue doing the inner work needed to heal more fully.

Releasing Difficult Feelings

The additional work Carolyn had to do to resolve the grip of her panic attacks was extensive. Once she stopped denying her internal experience, some very powerful and volatile emotions rose to the surface. While facing these feelings head-on eventually led to a great deal of healing, it was hard for her to admit the rage she was harboring toward her father, as well as her fury at her mother for her passivity. She also had to come to terms with the outrage she felt at being treated unfairly as a woman of color in a corporate environment. Lastly, she had to acknowledge her grief at being unsuccessful at forming meaningful relationships with men.

As she allowed herself to admit the depth and degree of her rage and grief, Carolyn was able to begin the work of resolving these emotional states. In time, she was able to facilitate further forgiveness between her inner abuser and abused. She was able to reestablish balance within herself as both parts took responsibility for their role in fueling the discord within her. This brought peace to the two and stopped the abusive inner dynamic that had been dominating her life. In the end, Carolyn recovered much of her health and was able to lead a happier and more fulfilling life.

It's important to note the role that forgiveness played in shifting the way in which the inner abuser and abused related to each other. By taking full responsibility for their actions and offering forgiveness to and accepting it from each other, both parts were free to change how they responded to the fear that arose whenever Carolyn was near her father.

Due to her father's refusal to acknowledge her experience, Carolyn was unable to truly forgive her father and heal the larger family issues. In relationships where incomplete forgiveness occurs, some of the members are expected to deny their experience, making conflict resolution impossible. When telling the truth is not a priority, confusion sets in as we are forced to suppress our "negative" emotions, such as anger and jealousy. By denying our emotions, we not only make discovering the truth behind them more difficult, we make alleviating the suffering they cause impossible.

As we saw with Carolyn, sometimes we find ourselves behaving in ways that maintain harmful dynamics within our relationships in an effort to protect ourselves or others and to avoid "rocking the boat." Unfortunately, this only makes the problem worse and paves the way for further harm to occur. It is true that the path to resolving conflict is not always a clear one, and that we may encounter obstacles along the way. People involved in conflict are not always willing to do the work needed to restore harmony. This is even more difficult when someone says they'll do the work, but are not being honest and only seek to further manipulate or control the situation. In these instances, it's up to us to decide what is best and how we can promote happiness and wellbeing for ourselves and others, rather than support—openly or through our silence—systems that cause harm.

The tools and support found in Coming to Peace help us confront our experience truthfully and completely, no matter how difficult it may be. This gives us the strength and understanding we need to pull ourselves out of harmful situations. It encourages us to forge our own path in the face of unfair systems or relationships, even if this goes against what's expected of us. Regardless of what others think or do, it is up to us to be truthful with ourselves about our experience and take responsibility for our situation. Being honest, even if we can only be honest with ourselves about our experience, is the most important element of changing difficult situations. As we will see in the next chapter, it is possible to free ourselves from harmful relationships without guilt or regret.

CHAPTER 10: BREAKING FREE FROM NEGATIVITY

"Stop identifying with the world created by your mind, and a new world will open up before you."

- Amma (Mata Amritanandamayi Devi)

Like the first rays of sunlight rising up to illuminate the day, an awareness of our authentic self slowly dawns when we engage in the Coming to Peace process. Through our self-discovery, we are able to see the ways in which we generate conflict, and to perceive the nature of our relationships. By looking more closely at our connections with others, we begin to understand why it is we stay in relationships that make us miserable, and open to the possibility of freeing ourselves from unhealthy patterns of behavior.

The price of staying in harmful relationships can be a hefty one. The reasons we remain in discontented relationships are often a mystery to us. We may not understand what binds us to another, or we may refuse to acknowledge the depth of our unhappiness for fear of having to make a change.

When the negative relationship is with a family member, it may feel unbearable or even wrong to acknowledge our unhappiness. We may make up stories or excuses about the root of our discontent, pretending it's something other than the relationship that's causing us to feel so unhappy.

Staying is something we may do because we believe that if we just do or say the right thing, we will finally succeed and our discontent will disintegrate. Or we may remain in the relationship out of sheer stubbornness, believing if we hold steady in the struggle to be happy, our ability to weather the storm will somehow show the world that we are strong and committed.

We may decide to remain in an unhealthy relationship because we don't want to admit that we can't fix it. Or we may fear being alone, and find it easier to disconnect from our discomfort using denial, numbing, addiction, or any other number of mechanisms designed to keep us from feeling our negative emotions and taking responsibility for our experience.

The problem is that by not acknowledging our situation and taking responsibility for the harm we are experiencing, we make ourselves helpless to change the situation. This creates a state of powerlessness within us where we are not actively making positive choices for ourselves, and we wind up staying in relationships in which our wellbeing is not a priority. By remaining in this state of powerlessness, we become vulnerable to being exploited. When we do not value our own happiness and wellbeing, it invites others to devalue us too.

The Importance of Happiness

Happiness is a key component to a fulfilling life. Even with the difficulties we all face at times, happiness is our natural state and we can always return to it. Unfortunately, many of us don't believe we deserve to be happy, or that we can put our wellbeing before another's without appearing selfish. This message is common among certain cultural and spiritual traditions, which de-emphasize the individual's happiness and emphasize the demand to give unconditionally to others as a form of enlightened service. However, if we give to another in a way that does not also preserve our happiness, we can become weakened physically, mentally, emotionally, and spiritually. To cope, we may resort to using denial or delusion, such as engaging in a pattern of martyrdom to stay in the service game and be a "good person."

When we take on a role to be in service to others, it's important that we put our wellbeing as equal to the wellbeing of the person we are serving. The reason for this is simple: If we do not preserve our own health and happiness, we cannot possibly stay the course on the path of service. We will become too burned out to help others. Giving without thought to our own wellbeing increases our risk of becoming depleted and creates an imbalance in the relationship.

Power imbalances are always a sign that an inappropriate exchange is occurring. For example, when we offer help to another in order to feel better about ourselves, we're using the act of giving or helping to mask or soothe a sense of inadequacy within us. This kind of service has a hidden agenda, which is to receive recognition. Instead of giving for the pure joy of it, we do so for a reward. We may become upset or even angry when we don't get our reward. In doing so, we entangle the person we are supposed to be serving in our personal drama. When we bind others to us in this way, we leech them of their power rather than leave them to enjoy the fruits of our kindness.

Simon

More often than not, failing to take care of ourselves creates a power imbalance in our relationships. This happens when there is a lack of clarity and conviction about what makes us truly happy, or it can be a reflection of our lack of belief that we deserve to be happy. This lack of clarity grows when we seek approval or love from someone who is duplicitous or is not truly interested in or capable of offering us love.

Simon, a wealthy man in his mid-fifties, was stuck in an abusive relationship with a beautiful young woman named Claudia. Claudia was intent on having Simon take care of her financially and emotionally. To get what she wanted from Simon, she would reject his efforts to please her at every turn, while telling him that she loved him and wanted him to be the "right man for her." Simon's response to Claudia's double message was to try harder to please her, offering her everything she wanted so that she would finally see him as Mr. Right.

Unfortunately for Simon, this was not his first relationship with a manipulative woman. He had been married three times before meeting Claudia, and each of his wives had used the same strategy of exacting resources from him. This long, grueling pattern of exploitation in the name of love had created a serious state of exhaustion, self-doubt, and despair in Simon.

What Simon did not understand is that his state of despair was due, in part, to his own actions. Unbeknownst to him, he had an internal dynamic where one part of his inner self had aligned with the unkindness of these women, while another part was withering in the face of that unkindness. Both parts had differing responses to the women in his life: one part viewed them as enemies, while the other felt they were allies. Simon was exhausted from the cruelty he was experiencing both externally and internally and this was manifesting as an autoimmune disorder.

Rooted in childhood, Simon's trouble with women started early as he desperately angled for his mother's affection. He is the youngest of three boys in a family that struggled to cope with the repeated absences of a father who was a famous movie star. To soothe the feelings of abandonment from her spouse, Simon's mother looked to her sons to give her what she wasn't getting from her husband. Simon and his brothers competed for her attention. Simon, in particular, was willing to do almost anything to get his mother's approval and ensure that his brothers did not.

For Simon, the relationship with his mother was a constant struggle as he worked tirelessly to give as much of himself as possible to ensure that she did not leave the way his father did, and to secure her love in the way he could not secure love from his father. The yearning for his mother's love was so strong that he viewed his mother loving his brothers more than him as a dire threat to his wellbeing. This pushed Simon to go beyond what might be considered normal limits in catering to his mother's whims. He did things for her to make sure her love was always focused on him.

Any hint of dissatisfaction by his mother stirred Simon to give more. His desperate need to keep her love focused on him blinded him to the fact that she was using her needs to keep his attention focused on her. This strategy was designed to "harvest" Simon's energy in order to assuage her emptiness and the sense of feeling unloved she felt from her husband's absence.

Later in life, when Simon entered into romantic relationships with women, he brought with him the desperation for love and willingness to do anything to get it that was the template of his relationship with his mother. When Simon came to me for help, he was struggling with a physical collapse that had no medical explanation.

As Simon and I began looking into his relationship with Claudia, he revealed to me that he paid her rent, "loaned" her money to keep her business afloat, and had cut ties with all of his friends that she did not like. Soon it became clear how their relationship was draining him on many different levels, and this left him feeling depressed and physically unwell. He also described previous relationships with women that followed a similar pattern of him giving everything and receiving little in return, leaving him feeling similarly unhappy and confused.

To better understand Simon's perspective on his relationship to his girlfriend, I asked him a series of questions. First, I asked him if he was happy in his current relationship, to which he replied that his girlfriend was beautiful. I posed the question several more times and his response was that he was sure he could never "get" such a beautiful woman, and that he liked it when other men saw him with her.

Eventually, Simon explained that it didn't matter whether he was happy because he was in a relationship with a beautiful woman—that was all that mattered to him. He felt that if he was seen with such a beautiful and exotic woman, other men would envy him, and this provided him with a sense of self-satisfaction. To Simon, having a beautiful woman on his arm made him feel validated and loved, no matter how demanding the relationship was.

When I pointed out the possibility that his body may not agree with his mind about being in a relationship with Claudia, Simon stopped short. He had never considered the possibility that his chronic over-giving could be the cause of his autoimmune illness. He was shocked to learn that his nagging symptoms might be due to the fact that he had been giving every ounce of himself, emotionally and financially, to the women in his life.

I asked Simon whether Claudia ever paid for dinners they shared and he said that she did not. When I asked if she ever did errands for him the way he did for her, he said she became angry if he asked her to do such things. Simon explained that Claudia needed him more than he needed her because she earned less money than him and she came from a broken home. He felt empowered by this dynamic of her leaning on him heavily for financial support because, in his mind, it secured him a place in her life.

When I asked Simon how he felt when Claudia got angry if he refused to meet her requests, he admitted that he rarely refused her. He explained that he always met her requests because not doing so would lead to a barrage of blame and scorn by her that would be too much rejection for him to bear. Again, he defended his girlfriend's behavior: she had suffered so much, so it was okay for her to make him suffer.

Victim-Perpetrator Inversion

After many years of counseling people, I have noticed the presence of certain patterns. Some are common, others more obscure, and still others repeat themselves with regularity. To make them easier to understand, I have named some of these patterns and attempted to explain how they work. I refer to one such pattern as the Victim-Perpetrator Inversion.

The Victim-Perpetrator Inversion is at play when the person in the perpetrator role (person who is harming another for their own benefit) inverts the dynamic by making it seem as though they are the victim. This was the case with Claudia and Simon. In relationships with this dynamic, the perpetrator (in this case, Claudia) assumes the role of the victim to manipulate their actual victim (in this case, Simon) in order to gain power. Power, in this sense, can be defined as energy, resources, attention, or time. A distinguishing characteristic of this pattern is that, in a previous relationship, the perpetrator was, in fact, the victim. The internalization of that victimization drives the dynamic of the Victim-Perpetrator Inversion in their future relationships.

The internalized victim part of the perpetrator seeks to fill the powerlessness experienced when they were originally violated. They do this by victimizing someone else in an attempt to fill the void of powerlessness inside, which causes the victim to direct energy and resources into the perpetrator. Not all victims in the Victim-Perpetrator Inversion become perpetrators, but all perpetrators have been victims.

This Victim-Perpetrator Inversion usually manifests with the perpetrator claiming that the victim has harmed them in some way. The result is the actual victim scrambles to try to alleviate the alleged damage by trying to find some way of appeasing the actual perpetrator, which is impossible since the victim has done nothing wrong. This dynamic can only occur if the victim accepts blame for the perpetrator's accusation. This is where it gets tricky. The willingness on the victim's part to believe that they are doing harm when they are not comes from an inner sense of powerlessness. What directs this sense of powerlessness is usually an internalized perpetrator within the victim, which was the case with Simon's relationship. At the heart of this pattern, there is always a power imbalance seeking correction. Unfortunately, it cannot be righted in this way.

Simon's girlfriend is an example of the victim who becomes a perpetrator. In Claudia's experience, she was the victim of a lack of love by her parents. The victim within her that evolved from the experience drove her to seek to fill the void left by her parents' unkindness by becoming a perpetrator and abusing Simon in an effort to assuage her sense of victimization. In this case, it was true that Claudia had suffered as a child from her parents' neglect; she truly was a victim of them. But it was her responsibility to heal those wounds and not use them as a weapon to manipulate and harm others. She failed to take that responsibility and, like Simon's mother, chose to use her wounds as a way to extract Simon's energy, resources, and power.

As we continued our work together, the Victim-Perpetrator Inversion in Simon's relationship with Claudia became more pronounced. In the rare moments when there was peace between them, she would disrupt the calm by picking a fight and pointing out ways in which he was not living up to her expectations. By making Simon responsible for her not being happy with him, she made herself out to be the victim and Simon the perpetrator in the situation. Rather than defend himself from her false assumption, Simon would react to her nitpicking by giving more of himself to her. Because he had no boundary to her dissatisfaction with him, he was unable to defend himself against her negative intention to take as much from him as she could. Simon's inability to defend himself against his girlfriend grew out of his unexamined willingness to do anything—including harm himself—in order to be loved.

The eagerness with which Simon would put his girlfriend's needs before his own so that she would love him created a split within him. One part of Simon was willing to continue to do whatever it took to please Claudia. The other part no longer wanted him to put her needs ahead of his, and was tired of the harm this was causing him. Simon's relationship with Claudia was a reflection of the inner conflict within him. The unresolved dynamics created by this internal split caused him to feel as though he deserved to be treated poorly, which allowed him to tolerate the unkind behavior of his girlfriend.

Simon's internal conflict also made it difficult for him to recognize his own unhappiness. He had become so numb to the effect of his own internal cruelty that he could not fathom the full effect of Claudia's cruelty. Because he wasn't making his own happiness a priority, Simon could not effectively defend himself against her negative intention toward him.

As he began connecting the dots between the cruelties Claudia doled out and his response to her and his resulting physical issues, Simon began to consider leaving the relationship in order to regain his health. When he told her that he wanted to leave, Claudia gathered up the clothes and other belongings he kept at her apartment, doused them with lighter fluid, and burned them to ashes in her backyard. Only then did Simon realize the depth and ferocity of her cruelty.

Even in the face of her malicious outburst, Simon struggled to leave Claudia. In exploring the causes for this paralysis, we found that there was a powerful conflict at play between the part of Simon that wanted to leave the relationship and the part that wanted to stay. The part of him that wanted to leave was exhausted and understood his girlfriend to be the enemy. But the part that wanted him to stay was allied with her cruelty. It was this abusive dynamic inside Simon that led him to participate in abusive external relationships.

The Inner Dynamic

To get to the root of the inner conflict that was causing Simon to repeatedly enter into abusive relationships, he participated in the Inner Coming to Peace process. With the help of a guided meditation, Simon established a relationship with his inner guidance that took the form of an old wise man. During the first session, he identified the feuding parts of himself as the "Rejecter" (R) and the "Collapsed" (C). The Collapsed was as afraid of the Rejecter as Simon was of women rejecting him. He perceived the Rejector as a splinter located in his throat and the Collapsed as a crushing feeling in his forehead, as if in a vice grip. The following conversation is one of many between the two parts during our sessions.

Session 1

Here is the first conversation that took place between the Collapsed and the Rejector:

Collapsed: *I don't like it when you are making my head hurt.*

Rejector: *Why should I care?*

Collapsed: *I don't know.*

Rejector: *It's about time you got it. No one cares about you. Who would ever care about a loser like you?*

Collapsed: *No one.*

Because the Collapsed was unable to have compassion for itself, I suggested that it sit in meditation with the Guide. The rest of the session was spent in meditation, and Simon was encouraged to take time to reflect on the Guide in this way until his next session.

The next two sessions were spent helping Simon develop greater compassion for himself in order to strengthen the Collapsed. It wasn't until Session 4 that the conversation between the Rejector and the Collapsed could resume. Here is what transpired:

Session 4

Collapsed: *Stop criticizing me.*

Rejector: *I can't stop. You have to get used to it, so when others reject you, you won't get hurt. We have to practice preemptively.*

Collapsed: *I appreciate the thought, but it's not helpful. You are hurting me more than anyone else would.*

Rejector: *Really?*

Collapsed: *Really. I'm not sure you're getting the full effect of what you've done to me with your criticism.*

Rejector: *Maybe I don't get it. But what's the big deal anyway?*

Collapsed: *The big deal is that I've been getting really hurt. It caused me to do things that hurt me even more. Your rejection has had serious consequences.*

Rejector: *Okay. I get it. I will try to understand what I have done.*

Collapsed: *It's good that you get it.*

These dialogues between the Rejecter and the Collapsed were the beginning of a long series of Inner Coming to Peace sessions in which the Rejecter repeatedly took responsibility for all the ways in which it had harmed the Collapsed. The Collapsed also admitted its role in failing to take full responsibility for its own wellbeing. It also took responsibility for "caving in" to the Rejecter.

As each part took responsibility for its role in the situation, they slowly pulled out of the abusive dynamic. This changed the template of abuse that originated from Simon's relationship with his mother. Resolving this inner conflict made him much less susceptible to his tendency to allow himself to be lulled by his girlfriend's double messages.

These Coming to Peace sessions helped heal the damage caused by the Rejecter and restore power to the Collapsed. As the Collapsed gained power, Simon started to feel more physically healthy. And as the Rejecter's voice softened, he no longer feared abandonment as strongly as he once had.

With his newfound inner strength, Simon felt less paralyzed at the thought of leaving Claudia. He began to realize the importance of the two internal parts of himself taking more responsibility for their experience. With this shift, Simon understood his primary responsibility was to continue to mend the damaged relationship between the Collapsed and the Rejecter, which had created so much strife for him.

Part of the reason it was so hard for Simon to leave his girlfriend was his concern for her wellbeing. After all, Claudia was a very troubled woman. While it was true that her childhood was difficult, Simon came to understand that it was the choices she was making as an adult, in relationship to her childhood trauma, that were exacerbating her suffering.

As Simon sought to make changes in their relationship, Claudia made it clear that she was unwilling to take responsibility for her choices. She became enraged when Simon suggested that she look at her situation in a new light rather than depending on him to make everything better for her. She blamed him for her problems and was unwilling to take responsibility for her cruelty, so she had no hope of healing. If Claudia had truly loved Simon and if she had allowed him to love her, their relationship might have created the secure container she needed to heal. Unfortunately, the power of unconditional love was not present in their relationship.

As it turned out, Claudia preferred the power she experienced by engaging in the Victim-Perpetrator Inversion, which enabled her to get others to take care of her while she was abusive to them. She wasn't interested in giving up this power by healing the wounded victim within her. She refused to do any work on herself and instead insisted that the unhealthy dynamic of their relationship continue.

Unlike his girlfriend, Simon had taken full responsibility for the way his internal conflict was informing his external conflict with others. Because he was willing to do this difficult work, Simon was able to free himself from an abusive relationship without causing harm to Claudia or himself. He was able to liberate himself from his pain and unhappiness without her permission. And he finally released himself from the harmful pattern of serving others in exchange for their love, a desperate pattern he had been trapped in since childhood.

When we tell the truth even about the most difficult aspects of relating to others and ourselves, we can understand the nature of our relationships and make clear choices about them. Sometimes, leaving a relationship that generates and fosters negativity is the right choice. Simon's experience gives hope to those of us wanting to break free from an abusive relationship. As we witnessed, we do not have to heal the other person, nor do we have to wait for the other person to heal before we can leave a harmful situation.

In the following chapter, we will focus on forgiveness and what further steps we can take to free ourselves from negativity and pain.

CHAPTER 11: UNDERSTANDING FORGIVENESS

"As I walked out the door toward the gate that would lead to my freedom, I knew if I didn't leave my bitterness and hatred behind, I'd still be in prison."

- Nelson Mandela

True forgiveness is serious business. To forgive or be forgiven is a complex and stirring process that requires each side to dig deeply in order to restore peace. To reach a place of true forgiveness, we must set our sights on the heart of the conflict and begin the necessary work of self-examination so that we may find and release our attachment to the offense. Only then can we truly be free from our pain.

When it comes to forgiveness, there's a tendency by both parties to rush toward the finish line. But forgiving another or our self is more akin to a journey than a race. While it's understandable that we would want to smooth over emotional wounds in order to reestablish the relationship, rushing to do so is a mistake. Unless everyone involved engages in the hard work behind true forgiveness, the relationship will forever be tainted by the offense. The relationship then bears the risk of becoming superficial, marked by compromise at best and hypocrisy at worst. Rushing to forgive creates a mask of neutrality behind which volatile and sometimes even destructive emotions loom. This can lead to a condition of incomplete forgiveness, as we saw with Carolyn and her father in Chapter 9.

True forgiveness is not easy, and depending on which side of the offense we are on, the work necessary to grant or receive it is markedly different. As we will see, "the offended" and "the offender," while both responsible for their part of the forgiveness process, have distinctly different roads ahead.

The Offended

If we've been hurt by someone and are in the position of granting forgiveness, the process is primarily one of release. Doing so allows us to move on from the offense and the harm it caused us, and prevents any further harm from occurring. But before we can do this, it's important to examine all the places inside us that remain attached to having been wounded.

The reasons for staying attached to an offense are unique to each of us. Some of us may not realize we are attached to the offense and the emotional wound caused by being wronged. Others of us are unclear about the effect the offense has had on us and, therefore, we're unable to let go of it. And still some of us are so angry at having been hurt that we decide to actively cultivate a grudge to punish the other person, which only binds us more permanently to our wound and the person who committed it.

But there is hope. By engaging the process of forgiveness in a serious and dedicated manner, we can actually begin to uncover these attachments so that we may heal and release them. It's only by participating in this process that we can reach an authentic experience of forgiveness.

For Carolyn (from Chapter 9), the desire she had for things to be better with her father caused her to bury the genuine feelings of anger she had in response to her father's rage and addiction to drugs. This contributed to her feelings of panic and anxiety. Often, when we rush to forgive without fully processing our feelings, the kind of imbalances Carolyn experienced occur within us, which can affect our health and wellbeing.

One of the best ways to determine where we are in relationship to the offense is simply to ask ourselves how we are feeling about it. If we're feeling angry and unable to move past that anger, then it's important to honor the reasons for our anger, rather than feeling badly for being mad. So often we are pressured to forgive prematurely by outside forces like family and friends who want things to be better quickly. But we also put pressure on ourselves because we want to move beyond the ordeal too. Yet pushing past our anger is not the solution. In order to truly reestablish peace, our best bet is to take a good look at our anger and try to discern what it is showing us, particularly any places where we are twisting away from ourselves in an attempt to make the situation appear better than it actually is for us in the moment.

By acknowledging our anger and feeling its presence, we have the opportunity to understand what it's trying to teach us about the situation. It informs us about what issues still need to be addressed. Once we do this, the anger will naturally shift on its own. In instances where we have become attached to the offense, it may feel impossible to forgive the person or group who has harmed us. In these cases, it is still important to accept our feelings and not feel badly for not being able to forgive yet.

When we remain in the dark about how we're feeling, our physical responses can serve as clues. For instance, we may feel highly irritated with the person who caused the offense, or we may avoid that person altogether. We may also experience some physical symptoms such as nausea, headaches, or digestive issues when we're around or even just thinking about the offender. These may all be signs pointing us to look more closely at the issue and what we need to do in order to genuinely heal from it.

Once we have dissected our reactions to the offense and are ready to grant forgiveness, we move on to the ultimate healing process of releasing the offender to the consequences of their actions. It goes without saying that this is often the most difficult part of the process, especially if we are determined to see them take responsibility for their behavior in a particular way. When we base our forgiveness on the actions of the other person, we remain tethered to them and the offense. It's only when we can let go of our attachment to the offender taking responsibility, and release them to the consequences of their actions, that the process of forgiveness can become one of liberation from the offender and the pain they caused us.

This last piece is particularly important for those of us wanting to forgive trespasses committed by someone we are no longer in contact with or who has died. In this way, we're able to free ourselves from the offender without their participation.

Through the process of forgiveness, we can reclaim the power we lost during the offense, giving ourselves the strength needed to heal our wounds on our own terms, without attachment to the outcome. This creates a true field of neutrality that buffers us from the person who wronged us, which must occur for forgiveness to take place. It is within this field that our attachments dissolve, and we can begin to move on with our life.

The Offender

As the person who is seeking forgiveness for causing harm to another, the process is one of engagement whereby we move toward the offense and take responsibility for our actions. This is often easier said than done. Requesting forgiveness is a humbling experience, but if we approach the process with sincerity in our intention and kindness in our heart, we may not only be granted the reprieve we desire, but likely will also learn deeply transformative lessons about ourselves.

For most, the thought of seeking forgiveness is daunting. Perhaps we don't fully understand the level of commitment required. Or, maybe we know full well what lies ahead and the inner work we must do, but feel paralyzed to take the steps needed to truly release the effect of our misdeed. So we choose not to take responsibility for our actions, making it harder for the person we hurt to forgive us, further ensnaring ourselves in the web of our own actions.

Our journey toward freedom starts when we choose to take full responsibility and examine the depths of our inner world to learn what is going on within us that allowed us to harm another. To begin, we must evaluate the root causes of the offending act, specifically our intentions, thoughts, and actions leading up to the violation. By following these back to their source, we'll have a better understanding as to why we committed the offense in the first place. This difficult process of self-examination, when engaged fully, can tell us more about ourselves than we could have ever known otherwise. And as we plumb further, clues about ourselves begin to surface, and the clarity they bring helps us shift our relationship to the root causes that lie behind the offending act.

It's not uncommon to be afraid to take responsibility for our actions because we fear the person we have hurt will blame us and make us feel worse. In fact, there are some of us who will do almost anything to avoid blame. That's because we are attaching shame to the act of doing something wrong. If we find ourselves justifying our behavior and actions to avoid blame, it's time to start examining these justifications. What we may discover is that old wounds from earlier in life are feeding our need to justify and defend against feeling ashamed. Thankfully, the process of forgiveness gives us the opportunity to confront and heal these wounds once and for all, releasing us from the need to constantly justify and defend ourselves.

By looking honestly at our behavior and thoughtfully considering the feedback we receive about our actions from others, we may mitigate or transform the consequences of the offense. This can only come about when we have genuinely recognized the harm we have caused. At this level of self-understanding, we are now ready to perform the next step in the process: self-forgiveness. Self-forgiveness is when we forgive ourselves for our infractions. It is not a rush to move past the hurt we've caused in an attempt to soothe our own discomfort. While it sounds simple, self-forgiveness is anything but. It requires us to hold a positive wish for our own happiness and freedom. Our ability to do this depends heavily on the way we feel about ourselves. If we are harboring negative ideas about ourselves and don't truly believe we deserve to be happy and free of emotional suffering, the road to self-forgiveness is likely going to be difficult. Alternatively, if we're able to feel compassion for ourselves and let go of our missteps with relative ease, more often than not it will be easier to practice self-forgiveness.

No matter which end of the self-forgiveness spectrum we are on, the process of seeking forgiveness will undoubtedly bring to light any areas that need our attention. In seeking forgiveness from another, we are given the opportunity to practice self-forgiveness and to evaluate how we treat ourselves. Then we can tap into the alchemy that becomes available to us when we practice true self-forgiveness and turn the poison of our offense into a flickering light of self-revelation. In doing so, we can finally leave behind our old black-and-white way of viewing the world with its enemies and allies, and step into a vibrant existence of peace and gratitude for the lessons our offense has taught us. From this illuminated vantage point, we experience a new sense of wholeness and interrelatedness with others that is at the heart of Coming to Peace and is the basis for true happiness.

Unfortunately, some of us remain trapped by our transgression because we are unable to practice self-forgiveness. Bound to the offending act, we continue to suffer from our actions. Another force that can keep us stuck is the mistaken belief that we must be forgiven by the person we have wronged in order to be released from the harm we caused them. But this is not the case. The truth of the matter is that it is our ability to forgive ourselves after we have stepped out of the shadows of denial and taken responsibility for our actions that liberates us from our misdeed, not the forgiveness of another.

Remembering that freedom from the offense is within our reach isn't easy when the person we have harmed refuses to grant us the forgiveness we so desperately desire. We may agonize over this but, in reality, they may not be able to forgive us because they haven't engaged in the inner work necessary to release their attachment to having been wounded. That was the case with Lucia, Juan's mother, in Chapter 6. She held a grudge against Juan for moving abroad to attend college. Lucia was unwilling to forgive Juan for her perceived harm by this move, so she remained stewing in her own anger.

Other cases are not so benign, such as when the offended person refuses to grant forgiveness with the intent to punish the person who harmed them, and actively builds grudges that solidify the offense. This practice of grudge-making is a trap—but not for the offender. Through grudge-making and refusing to forgive in order to punish, the offended person actually becomes an offender, using their wound to ensnare and harm far beyond the consequences of the original offense. This practice of holding grudges only causes more harm, especially for the person holding the grudge.

While grudge-holding and withholding forgiveness can be obstacles to our freedom, they are not the end of the road for those of us seeking forgiveness. When we examine our intentions, genuinely attempt to make amends, and forgive ourselves for our mistakes, we are well on our way to being free from our offense. Doing this difficult yet important work allows us to move on with our lives, even if the person we have harmed cannot or will not move on. It's also important to remember that, by holding the other person with compassion, we will not need them to rush to forgiveness to make us feel better. This stops the cycle of harm that can occur between us and others when connected by an offense.

Whether we are the offender or the offended, we have work to do to free ourselves from the negative effects of harmful incidents. Rushing to forgive is not the answer, nor is withholding forgiveness. Ultimately, our liberation from the offense depends on our actions alone. As we will see in the next chapter, the road to freedom is paved by our willingness to take responsibility for our actions and intentions.

CHAPTER 12: CYCLES OF HARM

"Once we find inner peace, any small bit of it, we feel much better ... Then whatever work we do to achieve outer peace ... comes from an effective place and does not create more turbulence and counter-reactions."

- Robert Thurman

To break free from the pull of negative patterns in our life, we must work to tell the truth of our experience and take responsibility for our actions whenever conflict arises. Only then can we be liberated from the suffering that ignoring our role in external conflicts creates. By examining the ways we act and react within our relationships, we are finally able to perceive aspects of ourselves that would have remained hidden from us otherwise. The information that we unearth about ourselves through interactions with others helps us break the negative patterns that are holding us back from a happier and more fulfilling life.

Coming to Peace is designed to interrupt the unexamined way in which most of us live our lives. This helps us "stop the tape" and review the circumstances that are leading us into conflict. Informed by a deeper knowledge of ourselves, we are better equipped to change the trajectory of our lives in a more positive direction. But make no mistake about it: Coming to Peace is not a miracle cure. To reap the rewards, we must put forth the effort required to break the harmful patterns that have dictated our lives up to this point. As we will witness in the following case study, when we remain unwilling to look at our motivations and at the consequences of our actions, we continue to cycle endlessly through one painful experience after another, remaining stuck and spinning in a cycle of harm.

Susan and Yvonne

When Susan and Yvonne came to see me for couples counseling surrounding issues with money, they were trapped in a vicious cycle ruled by their collective blame, anger, fear, and pain. They blamed each other for the problems that emerged as their fairytale courtship descended into a marriage of great strife, with one scuffle after another about money and sex. By the time they came to me for help, both were emotionally bruised and battered without even knowing why.

Blinded by the habit of looking at life through the sullied lenses of blame and self-victimization, neither Yvonne nor Susan could see how their refusal to take personal responsibility and their habit of hurling verbal arrows at each other were generating their marital problems. This trapped them in an abusive pattern in their relationship. As we saw with Simon in Chapter 10, cycles of blame and reactivity lead to a great deal of strife.

When teaching Depth Hypnosis, I instruct students to look for and identify the way in which people who have opposite internal reactions to the same kind of wounding in their birth families are attracted to each other as adults. We see this clearly with Susan and Yvonne, who share a similar childhood experience of instability due to the way their parents handled the family finances when they were young. As a result, both grew into adults with a complicated relationship to money and manner of meeting their material needs.

In Susan's birth family, her father created regular financial instability from numerous failed business attempts. Susan and her mother were forced to ride the rollercoaster that his entrepreneurial failings and mismanagement of money created. These monetary binge and bust cycles led to conflicts between Susan's parents and caused her quite a bit of stress. The ups and downs from her father's lack of success left Susan feeling vulnerable and exposed. As she grew older, she was determined to avoid experiencing this vulnerability ever again. To safeguard herself, she became a workaholic. While she managed her money effectively, she was also attached to the product of her hard work and enjoyed spending her wealth without worry. As long as she avoided the financial boom and bust cycles of her childhood, Susan felt safe. Thanks to her compulsion to work, she was guaranteed a steady stream of income with which to support her lifestyle.

Yvonne, on the other hand, came from a wealthy family with parents who, in her opinion, spent their fortune frivolously. Due to their irresponsible spending habits, they spent much of their time focused on acquiring more wealth. As a result, Yvonne felt both ignored and overwhelmed by the lack of love and attention from her parents. As she grew older, she became increasingly resentful and highly critical of them. Her relentless criticism of their spending habits angered her parents, which led to conflicts. Yvonne's response to her birth family was to trim her material needs to the bare necessities and earn very little money so that she could avoid becoming dependent on material needs. By doing so, she minimized any risk of being like them. This constriction around her needs enabled her to avoid the feeling of overwhelm she experienced from "having too much."

Though Susan and Yvonne had very different experiences growing up, the instability they experienced as children caused them both to feel a sense of overwhelm and powerlessness that carried into their adult lives. In response to that overwhelm, and to try to generate stability for themselves, they evolved different behavioral patterns in relation to their needs. Yvonne contracted in relationship to her needs, requiring very little, while Susan expanded, flooding her needs with material goods.

At the time of their marriage, Susan owned a house and held a high-paying job. She valued the material luxuries that her hard-earned salary afforded her, and she did not spare herself the pleasure of buying whatever she wanted. In particular, she enjoyed designer clothing, lavish jewelry, and expensive works of art. Yvonne, on the other hand, lived in a small studio apartment that she rented in a rough section of the city. She had a low-paying job, no savings, and was proud of not having accumulated many material things. This contrasting way of handling finances and material needs became the source of a major struggle in their relationship.

When people in relationship have contrasting reactions to similar circumstances, it's not an inherently bad thing. In fact, it can bring a creative element to the relationship, particularly when a couple is willing to examine the conflicts that arise. In this way, the dynamic can serve as an effective catalyst for self-inquiry and change. By dealing with conflict in an open and compassionate way, the relationship and the individuals in it are able to grow and thrive. However, if a person's reflex to vulnerability is to become defensive, then the dynamic quickly ignites into volatility.

The Struggle for Power

Disagreements over the way resources, such as money, are used is one of the most common reasons people end up in conflict. When conflicts arise over finances, especially between couples, it is usually pointing to something deeper that is going on in the relationship. Often the subtext of these conflicts is about where and how power should be distributed. In the social context, the relationship between money and power is clear: Those who have money are generally viewed as having power and those who do not are seen as being more or less powerless.

In interpersonal relationships, when one or both people have an internal sense of powerlessness they may try to combat this feeling by exerting their worldview or way of doing things in the relationship. This can lead to power struggles over things like how money will be distributed or spent. Whatever the context, power struggles are almost always about a need to feel in control. This was the case with Susan and Yvonne.

When they were courting, their opposing responses to the financial instability of their childhoods did not come into play. Both Yvonne and Susan had learned to hide the vulnerability they felt as children by developing a persona they presented to the world. In the beginning, each was attracted to the others' persona. Yvonne's persona was that of the nonconformist. To Susan, Yvonne appeared to be a freethinking individualist whose strong opinions she admired. Susan's persona was that of the avant-garde beauty. To Yvonne, Susan appeared to be an exotic flower whose mystery lay behind the beautiful clothes and jewelry she wore and her extensive knowledge of fine art.

As the novelty of their relationship wore off, Yvonne and Susan found themselves at odds. No longer enamored with each other's personas, they had to face their very real differences, and soon found themselves in a power struggle over the way they tried to create a sense of stability in their lives. To maintain power, Yvonne constricted the flow of spending in her life. She did this to avoid feeling out of control and exposed by the same excessive and irresponsible use of money she felt her birth family used. Yvonne judged her parents harshly for what she perceived to be an overindulgent lifestyle and she brought this same judgment to Susan and the way she chose to take care of her material needs.

Susan's solution to the bust and binge cycling of money that she experienced in her birth family was to maintain a steady, robust flow of it. This was how she tried to maintain power and avoid repeating the circumstances of her childhood, which had caused her so much distress. In this way, she attempted to guarantee against the starvation of her needs that occurred during the bust cycles of her youth. She also urged Yvonne to participate in this flow by earning more money and contributing more to the material aspects of their household.

Both Yvonne and Susan were trying to avoid the powerlessness they had felt as children as they fought each other over finances in the relationship. Each tried to assume control by asserting their worldview, which was what made them feel safe. On the surface, this looked like arguments over Susan's refusal to give up buying high-priced fine art and Yvonne's refusal to contribute to anything more than the basic household expenses. Their arguments escalated as Yvonne became more critical of Susan for her spending, and Susan refused to pay for Yvonne when they went on vacations or to expensive restaurants, which she had done earlier in the relationship.

Similarly, Susan and Yvonne had opposite strategies for managing their arguments. Susan overflowed with emotion, becoming upset and verbally expressive. This mimicked the way she flooded her needs with resources in response to the financial instability of her family. Yvonne's emotional response was to withhold and withdraw. This mimicked her method of constricting her needs in order to defend against what she viewed as her family's improprieties and her fear that having needs could cause her to feel hurt again. In their attempts to maintain control in their respective ways, Yvonne and Susan became destabilized. As the destabilization grew, so did the intensity of their arguments.

Abusive Cycles

Their relationship became increasingly toxic as each vied for power in the dynamic. In an effort to better understand their problems, they did a series of Inner Coming to Peace sessions and discovered that they had very similar internal dynamics. Both Susan and Yvonne found that they had an inner perpetrator and an inner victim that were locked in a dramatic battle. With the help of a guided meditation, Susan established a relationship with her wisdom that took the form of an oak tree and Yvonne established a relationship with her inner wisdom that took the form of a St. Bernard dog.

In Susan's Inner Coming to Peace sessions, she discovered a part of herself that she called the "Driver," which powered her workaholism. She identified another part as the "Sloth," which collapsed in exhaustion from the Driver's constant pushing and prodding. Susan was familiar with the Driver, as it was the ambitious hardworking part of her that she related to most. However, she had not been aware of the "Sloth" and how its collapse kept her in bed on weekends as she recovered from debilitating workweeks brought on by the relentless push of the Driver.

Yvonne discovered a part of herself she referred to as the "Crusher." The Crusher was determined not to have needs and ran the show with its criticism of Susan for her spending. It was also the source of the judgment of her parents. Yvonne found another part she called the "Crushed." This part was in response to the Crusher's demand that she have no needs, and tried to shrink to the point of needing as little as possible. This part also felt overwhelmed by the needs of others. Yvonne identified with the Crusher, feeling justified in her judgment of material excess, but she had not been aware of the Crushed, the part of her that sought to rid itself of any material needs in response to the pressure from the Crusher. This dynamic left Yvonne feeling frustrated and unsupported.

Both Yvonne and Susan were engaged in an abusive internal cycle. What characterizes this kind of cycle is having two internal aspects of the self at odds with each other—one attacks and the other collapses. The part that is attacking is acting as a perpetrator and the part that is collapsing is acting as the victim. When these two parts are able to reconcile, as we saw in Chapter 5 with Joel, a more balanced and peaceful internal dynamic arises. When the two parts are unable to reconcile, the internal environment of the person grows more self-destructive and unhealthy. This causes any external relationships affected by the internal dynamic to become increasingly hostile.

The internal dynamic of both Yvonne and Susan was abusive, as the dominant part of each of them beat up on the weaker part in an attempt to keep things under control. Both Yvonne and Susan identified with their dominant parts (the Crusher and the Driver) and liked the power they received when those dominant parts were in control. However, neither of them recognized when their weaker parts (the Crushed and the Sloth) took over after falling under the weight of the cruelty that was being generated by their dominant parts. This created a cycle of overworking and then collapsing for Susan, and a cycle of constricting and then withdrawing and behaving destructively for Yvonne. The couple's failure to recognize the weakened parts within them served to distance Susan and Yvonne from their vulnerability and allowed for their mutual internal abusive dynamic to continue to play out in their relationship with each other.

What this looked like was a pattern of attack and collapse with both Yvonne and Susan using anger to fuel their misaligned wills in an effort to get their own way. When Susan's Driver was in control, it would constantly badger Yvonne to get a better job and contribute more to the household. In response, Yvonne's Crushed would withdraw and withhold from Susan emotionally, financially, and sexually. Conversely, when Yvonne's Crusher was in control, Yvonne would criticize and pick fights with Susan over her spending, causing Susan to become so upset and drained that she would spend the entire day in bed. In this way, Yvonne's Crusher was treating Susan the same way it treated her own weakened internal part, the Crushed. Likewise, Susan's Driver treated Yvonne the same way it treated the Sloth.

Neither Susan nor Yvonne could see the effect their inner dynamic was having on themselves or each other. Both were so focused on trying to control the circumstances of the relationship to prevent re-experiencing the vulnerability they felt as children, they waged war on the weakened parts of themselves and each other. The tactics they used to shield themselves from the unkindness of their inner perpetrators continued to mirror one another, with them both pushing and attacking until they collapsed.

As the abusive inner dynamics continued to play out between them, their relationship grew more volatile. Susan's nagging turned into emotional, bullying displays, followed by punishments, such as not inviting Yvonne to join her for dinners or other social events. This led Yvonne to withdraw into an even more profound isolation, where she deprived herself of her needs and desires in order to punish Susan. From that place of deprivation, she would then lash out. For instance, once Susan returned home to find one of her newly purchased paintings covered with a towel. Another time, Yvonne had scribbled on a piece of paper and taped it to one of Susan's favorite pieces of art.

The Demise of a Marriage

In the end, Susan and Yvonne felt safest solidifying their power in the relationship by aligning with their inner perpetrators, rather than addressing the harm they were causing one another and themselves. The love they had for each other was not enough to make them change course. This is the path of war, and the only way to stop cultivating war is to take responsibility for engaging in battle in the first place. Because both women refused to take personal responsibility, they became heavily ensnared in cycles of harm, each taking turns as the perpetrator and the victim.

Ideally, when conflicts between intimate partners arise, they reveal underlying vulnerabilities. This discovery is huge because it serves as an opportunity for the partners to reach beyond the conflict in search of its root cause. In such cases, the love each person has for the other helps them overcome their reflexive positions and unhealthy behavioral patterns to try and understand the other's experience. As they encounter the pain the conflict is causing one another, they are able to gain a new perspective on their own pain and actions. This creates a shift in the way they relate to their respective vulnerability. As each person feels more accepted by the other, the connection between them deepens. However, when defense mechanisms are too strong or too laden with negativity, as was the case with Yvonne and Susan, achieving this strong bond is nearly impossible.

In Yvonne and Susan's case, had they chosen to do the work necessary to heal their relationship, they would have also healed themselves, freeing themselves from the harsh abusive patterns churning inside them. And had they been able to see what the conflict in their relationship was trying to show them about the imbalance inside themselves and the misery these imbalances were generating in their marriage, they could have seized the opportunity to move beyond the internal and external discomfort and shared a much more fulfilling and peaceful life together.

One of the primary reasons why Coming to Peace did not work for Susan and Yvonne, individually or as a couple, was their resistance to recognizing their vulnerability and refusal to take responsibility for their parts in the ever-present negative patterns of their relationship.

Ceasing Negative Patterns

The task of Coming to Peace, either with a couple or an entire group, is to break through self-justification by inviting everyone to tell the truth of their experience, particularly the damaging effects of another's actions. This will often motivate people to reconsider their harmful strategies. But when people are not truly interested in peace and understanding how it supports everyone, and prefer to focus on the power they can garner from their bids for control in their encounters with others, then peace becomes much more difficult to achieve. Unfortunately, many people are unable to break free from these repeating negative patterns of behavior that keep them locked into cycles that are harmful to both members. However, in relationships where love and compassion are cultivated, lasting change is possible. As the external conflict boils over, people who care deeply about each other are often motivated to see beyond their limited worldview and take responsibility for their actions as they seek to create harmony within the relationship and themselves.

Of course, it's not always easy to see beyond our internal struggles and the pain of our situation to be able to hear the other person clearly and without defensiveness. It is difficult to sit unflinchingly in our vulnerability. And it is precisely for this reason that I have included Yvonne and Susan as an example in this book. Even with tools to understand ourselves, and a sincere wish to solve a conflict, it's not always easy to see past our own blind spots and find resolution. This doesn't mean that resolution is impossible; it just means that the work of knowing ourselves and taking responsibility for our actions is an endeavor that we must commit to if we want our situation to change. Putting forth the time and effort needed to cultivate a practice of compassion and openness is an investment in our happiness. In the next chapter, we will discuss how we can generate more peace in our lives and transform our day-to-day interactions with others and ourselves.

SECTION V

COMING HOME TO PEACE

CHAPTER 13: CULTIVATING PEACE MOMENT TO MOMENT

"Every opportunity for kindness is an opportunity to warm our hearts. Every moment where we feel uplifted by the kindness of others is an opportunity too. All we need to do when these blessings come our way is to be aware of them, and stay with the experience, rather than moving on to the next thing."

- Thupten Jinpa, Ph.D.

Throughout this book we have discussed the many personal choices we can make that support the processes of Coming to Peace. We've seen how the teachings found in conflict can help us stay focused on our path to resolution, guiding our steps so that we may learn the lessons of conflict without being overwhelmed by them. We have also seen the results of not doing the work of understanding what conflict has to teach us and how this can perpetuate negative situations and generate difficult experiences.

Now is the time to put all that we have learned into action by actively generating a happier, more peaceful life for ourselves. The good news is this doesn't have to be hard. It all begins with noticing our thoughts.

Quieting the Mind

With every waking moment our minds are churning out thoughts. These thoughts may amuse, confuse, upset, or inspire us. When we begin to train our minds, we learn to become more present to what is happening in our lives. When observed, our thoughts no longer overrun us the way they do when we are not paying attention to them. Unobserved thoughts can lead us down a road where we're making conclusions that have no basis in reality, which can cause us to feel anxious, angry, or upset in some other way. Yet when we become aware of our thoughts, we can make choices about whether what we are thinking is useful or harmful and whether we want to ignore or react in response. This allows us to create more positive states of mind by literally choosing to engage more intentionally with thoughts that promote positivity within us, rather than those that cause us to feel badly.

Taking time each day to observe our thoughts and reflect on our state of being is an important part of connecting with our essential nature and developing a well-rounded, holistic perspective. Meditation is one practice that can be helpful in this endeavor. In its simplest form, meditation is the process of quieting our mind, and is a useful practice for observing our thoughts. While quieting the mind is a goal of meditation, it's not necessarily easy to attain. Rather, we benefit most from the practice of observing our thoughts.

As we become aware of our thoughts as they arise, and resist the urge to follow them willy-nilly, a funny thing happens: we begin to train our minds to slow down. Like a puppy on a leash, the unobserved mind tries to pull us in every direction. Yet with a little training and a lot of patience, our thoughts and emotions will learn to walk in step with us. By training ourselves to observe thoughts and emotions before reacting to them, we become more skillful at discerning which thoughts will serve us and which will hinder us. This gives us an opportunity to create more positive interactions in the world.

Of course, this is a pared down explanation of meditation and its benefits. If you are one of the millions of people who already practice meditation, then you know the benefits of having a regular practice. For those of you who would like to learn more, there are many excellent books on meditation and places that offer instruction. My goal here is not to teach you about meditation, but to emphasize the importance of taking the time to observe your thoughts, which is possible to do even if studying meditation doesn't resonate with you. Sitting quietly in nature or in whatever setting feels right to you can also be effective when done regularly.

Too often in our society we stop ourselves from doing something before we have the chance to benefit from it because we fear we are doing it incorrectly. Don't let this stop you from taking time to observe your states of physical and mental being. Remember, there is no right—or wrong— way to try to understand yourself. As long as you take the time to try to quiet your mind, you are doing the work needed to support your happiness and wellbeing. It is imperative that you do this in whatever way works best for you so that you feel inspired to continue your practice.

Once we begin regularly observing our thoughts, then we can practice quieting them as they arise. This isn't easy to do and can land us in some pretty interesting places. It's not uncommon in one moment to be ruminating over a heated exchange with a neighbor, and in the next to be fantasizing about an exotic vacation. Whether or not we realize it, these are the places we go to in our minds on a regular basis. As we look at our thoughts, we may begin to notice how quickly we form judgments about situations we know little or nothing about, or how easily we can get worked up over something that we are not directly involved in. Just letting the mind run with itself leads to these ideas that are not necessarily true in the moment, yet have us reacting to them as if they are real.

For instance, if someone rushes by us as we are exiting a building, squeezing past as we're about to move through the doorway, we may feel annoyed. If we let our thoughts continue on this track, we may conclude that this person is rude and selfish. Going further, we may even find ourselves becoming angry and having thoughts like, *Who does that jerk think he is?* On one level, we actually have no idea if the guy is a "jerk" or if he's selfish. He may have been having a personal emergency and had to rush out of the building to tend to it. On another level, even if his actions were purely selfish, we are only harming ourselves by continuing to think about the situation, which has already occurred and no longer affects us, beyond us thinking about it. Often, it's the habit of letting our thoughts run away with us without realizing what we're doing that lands us in a bad mood. But as we become more aware of our thoughts, we gain insights that will help us avoid these types of unnecessary, personally disruptive episodes with others.

The more we develop this practice, the easier it will be to notice our thoughts and automatic reactions as we relate to others. When we catch our reactions before acting on them, it gives us the space we need to choose more effective and positive actions in any given situation. One of the most exciting milestones in this practice is when we begin to notice how much more effective and less reactive we are in our interactions with others. As our inner awareness grows, we begin to experience a peace of mind that we couldn't have imagined possible.

Acting with Compassion

The practice of observing our thoughts has another benefit: it helps curtail our judgment of others. When our thoughts go unobserved, we tend to form snap judgments about everyone and everything. The problem is, these judgments often have no basis in reality. Consider the following situation: We're standing on the sidewalk when we notice a policeman talking to a young man about fifty feet away. Our mind quickly jumps in and devises a scenario for what is happening. If we have a favorable opinion of the police, we may think the officer is helping the young man. But if we have a negative opinion of the police, we may think he's hassling the young man.

The truth is, we have no idea what is happening in that situation. Our minds create these types of misinformed scenarios constantly, and our reactions tend to be much stronger when we're making a conclusion about someone we know. In fact, it's fairly common to have habitual judgments about our family members and friends that keep us stuck in old ways of relating to them. An important part of steering clear of conflict is to examine our habitual ways of thinking about others.

As we become more conscious of our thoughts, judgments, and automatic reactions, we may begin to notice unkind thoughts that we have toward ourselves. It is true that self-compassion is a concept many of us struggle to embrace. If we have difficulty being compassionate toward ourselves, it's important that we pay close attention to any negative thoughts that are aimed at the self, such as judgments like, "I'm no good," "I'm stupid," or "I always mess everything up."

When these thoughts occur, we simply treat them like we would negative thoughts about others. First, we notice them and stop ourselves from following them to their negative conclusions. Then, we actively generate positive thoughts about ourselves to counteract those initial negative thoughts. For instance, if you think that you are no good, consciously make an effort to think of yourself as good. By thinking about good things you have done, even if they seem small or insignificant, you can get your thoughts back on a positive path and prevent yourself from spiraling down into a negative mental state.

Making the effort to counteract negative thoughts with positive ones in order to cultivate self-compassion cannot be stressed enough; it is the only way to interrupt the process of self-harm that occurs when we think of ourselves negatively. Embarking on this practice of self-compassion may even bring to light parts of ourselves that are in conflict and in need of Inner Coming to Peace.

As we develop more awareness of what's going on in our minds, we will naturally engage with others and ourselves in kinder, more considerate ways. As that awareness spreads to our speech—the words we use, our tone, and the information we choose to communicate—we will feel more in control of our experience and more at ease with others. Of course, this does not mean withholding our opinion. Rather, it means weighing the pros and cons of giving our opinion and then doing so in a way that takes the other person's experience into consideration. This helps foster behavior that is kind and compassionate to others as well as ourselves. The practice of observing our thoughts and training ourselves to be less reactive to those thoughts will help us communicate more carefully, clearly, and effectively. This will go a long way toward creating peace and happiness in our life.

Cultivating Positive Intention

Positive intention is the deliberate generation of thoughts and actions that are constructive and uplifting, rather than unhelpful or destructive. It is the movement toward happiness and wholeness. There are many ways to increase positive intention in our day-to-day lives; we just have to work on developing certain qualities of mind and heart.

One set of principles that I've found helpful and easy to adapt into a regular practice is drawn from Buddhist philosophy and is called the Four Immeasurables. For Buddhists, the Four Immeasurables are part of a larger spiritual practice that can be helpful and rewarding. However, in this book, I'm pointing to them in a secular, non-dogmatic way, as they can be applied by anyone for great personal benefit. These principles include cultivating, usually through a series of meditations, equanimity, loving-kindness, compassion, and joy.

The Four Immeasurables provide a kind of map for generating inner peace. The first Immeasurable, equanimity, challenges us to remain present with whatever is happening in our life without aversion, attachment, or anger. Developing a practice of equanimity helps us see others' priorities as equal to our own and their experience as important as our own. Attaining equanimity lessens our attachments and aversions, giving us more breathing room to consider other possibilities, rather than get hung up on one particular outcome.

The second Immeasurable, loving-kindness, invites us to live life with a more open, loving heart, and to carry the wish for everyone, including ourselves, to experience peace and to be free of hardship. In Buddhist practice, the wish for loving-kindness is first offered to oneself, and then to others. At first glance, offering this kindness to our self before another may seem selfish, but it's not selfish at all. As we have seen in the Coming to Peace processes, there cannot be peace in our external relationships unless there is peace within us.

If we have trouble offering loving-kindness to ourselves, we can begin work right away to resolve this inner conflict before it manifests into problems in our relationships. Trusting our own positive intention toward ourselves also helps us take responsibility appropriately without the fear that we will blame ourselves for having acted in a way that led us into conflict.

The third Immeasurable, compassion, encourages us to be benevolent toward ourselves and others. When we approach all situations with compassion, even those where negative intention is present, we do not fear judgment. Unlike loving-kindness, which is a general wish for everyone to be happy, compassion is more active, as it wades into the causes of suffering. With the practice of compassion, we approach conflict, or the suffering it causes, with the wish that everyone involved be free from their pain.

Ideally, what emerges when we work actively with the first three Immeasurables is the experience of the fourth: joy. This kind of joy is spontaneous and consistent and not dependent upon the actions of others or upon circumstances. One way to generate joy is to practice empathetic joy for others. This means looking for opportunities to be truly happy for another's good fortune. We can also practice having gratitude for our own good fortune. Both of these practices lead us closer to the experience of spontaneous joy on an ongoing basis.

In order to cultivate these principles in your daily life, simply sit and contemplate them, paying attention to your thoughts and also your actions in relation to these principles. When practiced regularly, your sense of internal harmony will grow and your relationships will blossom.

What we will inevitably learn through our efforts to cultivate peace is that we are all just trying to find happiness, however graceless that may look at times. By learning to observe our thoughts and cultivate positive intention, we will find ourselves better able to navigate situations where the potential for conflict arises. In the times when we do become entangled with another through conflict, we have a clearer pathway out. And should someone we are at odds with refuse to participate in the resolution process, we can do the work to resolve the issue within ourselves, walking away from the experience with any lessons the conflict had to teach us.

Each and every one of us has an astounding capacity to generate harmony within ourselves and carry it out into the world. I see it daily with my clients and students, some of whom have overcome harsh personal histories. It's not always easy, and certainly requires continued commitment, but if we do our best to put these practices to work every day, we will create inner and outer peace in our lives.

CHAPTER 14: CHOOSING PEACE

"If we have no peace, it is because we have forgotten that we belong to each other."

- Mother Teresa

As we finally settle into the awareness that there is an uninterrupted connection between our internal and external experience, we start to make a shift from understanding the concept of wholeness and interconnectedness on an intellectual level and begin to experience it more directly in our daily lives.

By learning to look past the surface level of conflict and the monotony of "he said, she said," a clearer view of the self begins to emerge on our quest for meaning. Steadily, we find ourselves more in control of our life, of our reactions and emotions, and this leads to a deeper sense of peace. With simple contemplative practices like meditation to watch our thoughts, we begin to recognize our automatic responses and become more open to tracking what arises from those responses to their roots within us. From this place of greater awareness of our internal thought processes, we are able to open up to our truth.

As we have seen through many of the case studies in this book, each person must tell the full truth of their experience in order to resolve conflict. When there is room for every single person to tell their truth, it creates trust. And as each person listens carefully to the experiences of everyone else in the group, a field of compassion emerges. This is not to say that getting to this place of trust and compassion is comfortable or easy. Often there are hurt feelings, anger, and other strong reactions that must be worked through before we can really listen to the other side of a conflict. Sometimes, it's just not possible to achieve resolution because one or more of the people in conflict are unable to get past these stuck places within themselves. When this happens, it is okay to accept the situation for what it is and to not feel as though we need to do more to bring the conflict to a formal resolution. Yet, even if we don't get the closure we had hoped for, we can still learn what the situation has to teach us and focus on bringing about peace within ourselves.

Despite the difficulties we will face at times, by taking the slow and steady steps necessary to get through the mire of obstacles that present themselves in conflict, we grant ourselves the priceless opportunity to make a profound change in our life. It may take many passes of the talking stick listening to each person's experience again and again, before we can actually *hear* what they are saying without having a personal reaction to it. Yet, as we take our chance at expressing our truth, and listen to others express theirs, it gets easier. We start to actually hear them and they start to hear us.

So many of our problems arise from not listening—the ancient Hawaiians understood this well and employed their ho'oponopono practices to help people really hear each other. If we want to heal our wounds, we have to commit to sitting and listening no matter how long it takes. We have to remain patient with the process, as it is the key to deactivating our strong emotional reactions that make us want to fight or run away from our problems. As we begin to feel more grounded, we calm down. Then, even if we still don't like what the other person is saying, it no longer has the powerful effect on us as it did in the beginning. And it is in this moment, when we are able to be present with what others are saying to us while also holding the truth of our own experience without reactivity, that we can see the situation with greater clarity and understanding.

When we no longer feel the need to defend our position because it's viewed as equal to others' in the Coming to Peace circle, we can embrace this opportunity to determine whether our observations about the conflict are correct. We may notice that we were mistaken in some of our perceptions. Or, we may find that we were correct about our assumptions and gain a better understanding of what was causing the other person to be mistaken as a result. Often what we find is that both sides are a little bit right and a little bit wrong.

Whether the conflict is within a community, family, couple, or the self, each and every person or part of the self must be allowed to tell and follow their truth even if doing so means sparking a conflict. If the conflict is well managed, it will give way to understanding. When we do not fear telling our truth—or being wrong—it's easier to feel compassion for ourselves and for others affected by the conflict. When compassion is fostered in all our relationships—externally and internally—it makes it possible for all parties to take full responsibility and to be honest about their experience. When there is enough space for everyone to speak without being cut off, trust takes root. What begins to arise is a less defensive atmosphere, one of mutual respect where the needs of all are genuinely considered without requiring anyone to deny their individual experience. It allows everyone to explore the situation before jumping to conclusions or automatically arguing their point of view. In this environment, it is easier and more natural to make choices toward mutual wellbeing and peace, rather than enforcing choices that support the wellbeing of a few. The result is far fewer conflicts.

As we have seen, conflict is a powerful teacher that shows us where we are out of balance and exactly where we need to work to come into harmony. If we remember that everyone is a teacher to us, we can approach our experience and our lives with a sense of discovery. If we hold the view that everything and everyone is giving us information about our deeper self, we are less likely to hide behind the defensive patterns that prevent us from deeply knowing ourselves and others.

When we make a priority of understanding who we are through our relationships with others, we begin to trust that our unhappiness—and even our anger—is showing us where we are out of balance. This keeps us from trying to deny or defend. It also prevents us from refusing to allow others to trust and know their experience and from forming or participating in unjust societal, familial, professional, or religious structures that concentrate power, resources, and energy in the hands of a few. This is why it is so important to listen to our experience, however difficult it may be. The South Africans understood this fact as they formed the Truth and Reconciliation Commission, informed by the indigenous practices of *ubuntu*. They were seeking to lay bare the truth of the loss and grief that the atrocities of torture and murder committed during Apartheid generated in their communities. They understood that disagreements about mundane issues could not be addressed until people's deep-seated grief was expressed and acknowledged as fully as possible within the parameters of the Commission's hearings.

The founders of the Iroquois League also understood the importance of listening to the truths of those who lost their loved ones at the hands of others as they developed the tradition of the Caucus. The Caucus was designed to interrupt the destructive blood feuds that emerged when those who were wronged sought vengeance. By allowing their suffering to be fully expressed, the truth of their experiences brought the reality of the situation to life for the perpetrators in a way that grief buried in further brutality could not. In this way, relationships could be built on the ground of truth and harmony, rather than the perilousness of hatred, resentment, and denial.

In many ways, the practices of Coming to Peace are easy. They require us to look honestly at ourselves, examining our actions and motivations even as we review the actions of others. They encourage us to be watchful of our intentions and develop positive states of mind. When we become fluent at observing ourselves and opening to the experiences of others, we begin to feel a greater connectedness to the people we love, as well as people we don't know, and even those we don't like very much. And this sense of connection does not stop there. It expands out to people with different backgrounds from our own, different religions, ethnicities, political views, and lifestyles, and continues on to include all the creatures of the earth and the earth itself.

It is within this level of connectedness, this fellowship of sentience, that we experience true happiness. Freedom from the misery of "me, me, me" comes only when we are able to expand our hearts and minds to the point of holding our own truth while also considering the truth of others, including those hard-to-hear truths about the way we are hurting others. Once we reach this expanded place, we cannot help but become more caring in the way we treat others—our neighbors, other species, and the planet—as well as ourselves, and that's when we truly align with our essential nature, the peace inherent in each of us.

Every meal is an opportunity to contemplate and celebrate our connection to all of life. Consider the plants and animals that provide us with food and the people who tend and harvest them. There are also the people who transport the food to market, the people who built the trucks, planes, and trains that the food traveled on en route to the grocery store, as well as the people who provided the gas and oil needed to fuel those vessels. Then there are the people working in the store that maintain the produce, man the registers, and bag the groceries, even helping us out to our car if needed. And of course, there's the earth, which provides the soil, sunlight, water, wind, and fire required to create and prepare our food. When we think of every possible person and element involved in the production of just one meal, we quickly realize how undeniably connected we are to everyone and everything.

Now is an exciting and remarkable time on the planet, yet it is also a delicate one. As we continue to grow in number and intellect, it is more important than ever for us to develop our capacity for caring, compassion, and consideration. In this day and age, we have an abundance of choices, from what we buy to whom we love and how we treat each other. We can choose to dominate the earth and all of its inhabitants and resources, leaving an irreversible footprint on the planet, or we can choose to tread lightly, taking conscious footsteps with our thoughts, words, and actions, so that we may remain connected to our essential nature and the feeling of wholeness that connection brings.

Coming to Peace is a steppingstone on the path to peace, a path that is personal and unique to each of us. For me, it was the harmony in nature I experienced as a child that propelled me to appreciate peace as our natural state of being. It is something we can always access if we remain open to it. After decades of watching the earth and the ever-present interconnectivity of its species, elements, and cycling seasons, I have come to understand that if any one system fails, we are all in danger of failing. It is for this reason that I believe peace is not an option; it is a necessity. By working to further the happiness and wellbeing of others and ourselves, we are able to create the harmonious existence that we have been searching for all along.

ACKNOWLEDGMENTS

I feel blessed to have been able to discover the forces of consciousness in this lifetime. They have guided me both in my own development and in the development of this book. They have brought together the many factors which contribute to the message of this book and which have allowed me to offer it to you.

There are many people who have helped make this book possible. I would like to thank Laura Chandler, who has taught me—or who persists in trying to teach me—diligence, patience, and perseverance; Thupten Jinpa, who has offered me clarity, insight, and method; and Robert Thurman, who has brought me inspiration, hope, and reassurance. And I would like to thank the many teachers in many forms who have so consistently and readily offered guideposts toward a larger possibility. I would also like to thank my students who have taught me so much and who provided the prism through which the work of *Coming to Peace* could be discerned.

This book would not have been possible without the assistance of Cody Humston, whose infinite patience and good humor has always been such a balm to me; Simone Sandy Kershner, whose attention to detail and elephant memory keep everything organized so that we can continue to grow together; and Sherri Serino, whose loyalty and willingness to go the extra mile has offered help in the hardest times. These three people have worked so hard to support the Sacred Stream and *Coming to Peace,* and without them the work would not continue.

ACKNOWLEDGMENTS

I owe a huge thank you to Melanie Robins, whose vision, organization, and editing skills contributed greatly to this book. A special thank you goes to Andreas Ramos for his expertise and generosity of time and spirit. I would also like to thank the artists who lent their vision and skill to creating the book itself: Deborah Hall, who contributed the cover photo and Catherine Marick who did the cover design. And finally, I want to express my gratitude to the many people who gave their support, feedback, and encouragement throughout the writing of this book.

NOTES

Chapter 1: The Roots of Coming to Peace

1. H.H. the Dalai Lama and Howard Cutler, introduction to *The Art of Happiness* (Norwalk, CT: The Easton Press, 1998), x.

2. Elizabeth Kolbert, *The Sixth Extinction: An Unnatural History* (New York: Henry Holt and Company, 2014), 3.

3. For more information about Depth Hypnosis, visit depthhypnosis.com.

4. Thupten Jinpa, introduction to *A Fearless Heart: How the Courage to be Compassionate Can Change Our Lives* (New York: Avery, 2015), xxv.

5. Chade-Meng Tan, *Search Inside Yourself: The Unexpected Path to Achieving Success, Happiness (and World Peace)* (New York: HarperOne, 2014), 4.

6. Thupten Jinpa, introduction to *A Fearless Heart: How the Courage to be Compassionate Can Change Our Lives* (New York: Avery, 2015), xxvi.

7. For a more in-depth teaching of The Four Noble Truths, see H.H. the Dalai Lama, *The Four Noble Truths* (London: Thorsons, 1998).

8. Lawlor, Robert, *Voices of the First Day* (Rochester, VT: Inner Traditions International, Ltd., 1991), 18.

9. "Port Elizabeth Municipality v Various Occupiers (CCT 53/03) [2004] ZACC 7; 2005 (1) SA 217 (CC); 2004 (12) BCLR 1268 (CC). (1 October 2004)," *Saflii.org*, 2004, accessed October 13, 2014, http://www.saflii.org/za/cases/ZACC/2004/7.html#fn36.

10. E.K. Yamamoto, "Race Apologies," *The Journal of Gender, Race & Justice* 1 (1997): 52.

11. "H.Con.Res. 331—100th Congress: A concurrent resolution to acknowledge the contribution of the Iroquois Confederacy of Nations to the ...," *GovTrack.us*, 1988, accessed November 3, 2014, https://www.govtrack.us/congress/bills/100/hconres331.

12. Ibid.

13. Jack Weatherford, *Indian Givers: How Native American Transformed the World* (New York: Ballantine Books, 1988), 135.

14. Ibid., 138.

15. "Election of Pine Tree Chiefs," *Constitution of the Iroquois Nations*, accessed November 23, 2014, http://cscie12.dce.harvard.edu/ssi/iroquois/version2/3.shtml.

16. H.W. Schroeder, "The Tree of Peace: Symbolic and Spiritual Values of the White Pine," (In proceedings of the White Pine Symposium (73-83), Duluth, MN, Sept. 16-18, 1992), accessed November 23, 2014, https://www.treesearch.fs.fed.us/pubs/13474.

17. Jon Parmenter, "Introduction," *The Edge of the Woods: Iroquoia, 1534-1701* (Michigan State University Press, 2010), xxvii-2, JSTOR, accessed November 23, 2014, http://www.jstor.org/stable/10.14321/j.ctt130hjr7.

18. Manu Meyer, "To Set Right–Ho'oponopono, A Native Hawaiian Way of Peacemaking," *The Compleat Lawyer* 30 (1995): 31, accessed October 12, 2016, http://www.narf.org/nill/documents/peacemaking/1995-meyer-to-set-right.pdf.

19. Mary Kawena Pukui and Samuel H. Elbert, *Hawaiian Dictionary, Revised & Enlarged Edition* (Honolulu: University of Hawaii Press, 1986), 340-341.

20. Ibid.

21. Manu Meyer, "To Set Right–Ho'oponopono, A Native Hawaiian Way of Peacemaking," *The Compleat Lawyer* 30 (1995): 31.

22. Charlotte Berney, *Fundamentals of Hawaiian Mysticism* (Berkeley, CA: Crossing Press, 2000), 21.

23. Manu Meyer, "To Set Right–Ho'oponopono, A Native Hawaiian Way of Peacemaking," *The Compleat Lawyer* 30 (1995): 31.

24. Manu Meyer, "To Set Right–Ho'oponopono, A Native Hawaiian Way of Peacemaking," *The Compleat Lawyer* 30 (1995): 30.

25. Ibid.

26. Mary Kawena Pukui, E.W. Haertig, and Catherine A. Lee, *Nana I Ke Kumu (Look to the Source)*, Vol. 1 (Honolulu: Hui Hanai, 1983), 60.

27. Ibid.

28. E. Victoria Shook, *Ho'oponopono: Contemporary Uses of a Hawaiian Problem-Solving Process* (Honolulu: University of Hawaii Press, 1986), 11.

29. Andrew J. Hosmanek, "Cutting the Cord: Ho'oponopono and Hawaiian Restorative Justice in the Criminal Law Context," *Pepperdine Dispute Resolution Law Journal* 5, no. 2 (2005): 365, accessed October 13, 2014, http://digitalcommons.pepperdine.edu/cgi/viewcontent.cgi?article=1106&context=drlj.

30. E. Victoria Shook, *Ho'oponopono: Contemporary Uses of a Hawaiian Problem-Solving Process* (Honolulu: University of Hawaii Press, 1986), 11.

31. Ibid.

32. Manu Meyer, "To Set Right–Ho'oponopono, A Native Hawaiian Way of Peacemaking," *The Compleat Lawyer* 30 (1995): 31.

33. "The History of Huna." *Huna.com*, accessed November 14, 2014, http://www.huna.com/history-hawaiian-healing-spiritual-teachings.

34. Andrew J. Hosmanek, "Cutting the Cord: Ho'oponopono and Hawaiian Restorative Justice in the Criminal Law Context," *Pepperdine Dispute Resolution Law Journal* 5, no. 2 (2005): 359.

35. Rob Perez, "Hawaiians at risk: Healing efforts return to roots," *Honolulu Star- Advisor*, accessed January 11, 2016, http://www.staradvertiser.com/2016/01/11/hawaii-news/hawaiians-at-risk-healing-efforts-return-to-roots.

Chapter 3: Building a Foundation for Peace

1. "Smudging and the Four Sacred Medicines," *Dancing to Eagle Spirit Society*, accessed December 3, 2014, http://www.dancingtoeaglespiritsociety.org/medicines.php.

2. Rita Robinson, *Exploring Native American Wisdom*, Exploring (Franklin Lakes, NJ: Career Press, 2008), 295.

Chapter 5: Understanding the Self

1. Ruth Snowden, *Teach Yourself Freud*, Teach Yourself: History & Politics (New York: McGraw-Hill, 2006), 105–107.

2. Charlotte Berney, *Fundamentals of Hawaiian Mysticism* (Berkeley, CA: Crossing Press, 2000), 38-44, 48-50.

3. For more about how the parts of the self can have experience life differently, read "Sub-Personalities: Who's Calling Shots?" at http://www.huffingtonpost.com/natasha-dern/sub-personalities-whos-ca_b_447845.html.

4. John Rowan, *Discover Your Subpersonalities: Our Inner World and the People In It* (Abingdon, England: Routledge, 1993), 131.

5. Roberto Assagioli, *Psychosynthesis: A Collection of Basic Writings* (Amherst, MA: Synthesis Center, 2000), 5-7.

Chapter 8: Dealing With Difficult Emotions

1. Steven J.C. Gaulin and Donald H. McBurney, *Evolutionary Psychology*, 2nd ed. (London: Pearson, 2003), 121-142.

2. Editors of Encyclopaedia Britannica, "Defense Mechanism," Human Psychology, accessed October 28, 2014, https://www.britannica.com/topic/defense-mechanism.

3. C.G. Jung, *Psychology and Religion: West and East*, Collected Works of C. G. Jung, Vol. 11. (Princeton, NJ: Princeton University Press, 1970), 131.

ABOUT THE AUTHORS

Isa Gucciardi, Ph.D.

In the mid-nineties, Isa began developing Depth Hypnosis as she entered into clinical practice. Her studies, both in academia and in the field, of cultural and linguistic anthropology, comparative religion, and transpersonal psychology formed the basis of her approach with clients and students. As the body of work that grew out of her clinical practice became larger, she began teaching others so that more people could benefit from the techniques she had developed. In order to accommodate the number of classes that grew out of this process, she co-founded the Foundation of the Sacred Stream, which is now a school for consciousness studies in Berkeley, California, serving hundreds of students each year.

Isa teaches and speaks nationally and internationally, and she has published numerous articles, podcast episodes, and videos, and the book *Return to the Great Mother*. She maintains a private practice with institutions and individuals in Depth Hypnosis and Coming to Peace processes. Isa speaks five languages and has lived in eleven countries. She is the mother of two children and lives with her partner in San Francisco.

Laura Chandler

Laura Chandler is a writer, poet, and award-winning songwriter. She has worked in publishing, music and video production, and alternative therapy. Laura is the Executive Director of the Foundation of the Sacred Stream and is lead teacher for many of its classes. She has published numerous articles and her music has appeared in film and television.

Made in the USA
Columbia, SC
12 July 2017